UNPACKING "CHUCK"

THE TV SERIES INTERPRETED

by G. Walter Bush

To Ryan for watching-

To Kendall for listening-

To Kristen for reading and illustrating.

TABLE OF CONTENTS

PREFACE

I came late to the "Chuck" party. In fact, I didn't watch my first episode until nearly two years after the series was canceled by NBC. My son was watching the series on Netflix, and I casually viewed portions of a few episodes strewn throughout Season 1 while dropping in and out. I became intrigued with the relative sophistication of the show and found myself starting to analyze it. Not only did it blend comedy with drama and mystery in a unique manner, but I observed figurative elements in the text lacking in most network series, with the visual aspects just as crucial to interpretation as the script. I decided to go back to the start of the series and watch the episodes consecutively. The more deeply I scrutinized the audio-visual text, the more densely layered and inter-connected I found it. In that respect, it reminded me of the process of researching my master's thesis on Ridley Scott's "Blade Runner."

Ultimately, I decided to write a literary analysis "unpacking" the text of the series, thus the name of the book. However, as funny or mysterious as some facets of the show are, this volume is not going to focus directly on interpreting its comic or espionage aspects; the sheer size of the task requires narrowing the scope to the series' dramatic elements. Within this limited scope, the analysis will be fairly comprehensive. Chapters address all five seasons and attention is given to each of the major dramatic characters. In rough terms, about half of the book is Chuck and Sarah-centric (especially the early chapters, given the focus of the Seasons 1 & 2 text) and the other half not. The content is also selective, not exhaustive. I've concerned myself with topics I find most profound, ambiguous, or simply interesting. Since even some dramatic elements will not be covered, the book may perhaps best be described as a collection of critical or analytic readings. Some readings are structured around specific episodes or arcs while others are organized around literary devices or characters. Regardless of the structure, readings are developed with detail and oftentimes include close readings of ambiguous scenes.

This book is chiefly intended for the "Chuck" enthusiast, one who comes to the text possessing at least a basic grasp of the entire series. Still, it is not a blog. The primary goal is to interpret aspects of the series in as objective a manner as possible, not comment on or evaluate them. Moreover, the interpretational approach will generally emphasize letting the text interpret itself with only occasional references to elements outside the text. Spoiler alert: readers who have not finished the series may wish to do so before reading further. The analyses are periodically retrospective in nature, with elements from later seasons/episodes in the series used to inform interpretations of earlier episodes, starting with the very first chapter.

Regardless of the degree to which the reader concurs with my conclusions, my hope is that this book will serve as a worthy addition to the ongoing "Chuck" conversation and bolster interest in a series that remains worth thinking and talking about. If you find this volume insightful, I would be grateful for a positive review posted on Amazon! And please take a moment to like the Unpacking "Chuck" Facebook page!

- G.Walter Bush

CHAPTER 1:

Water Lillies

It might seem most logical to launch even a selective literary analysis of a TV series with a discussion of the show's pilot. While the first episode of "Chuck" certainly provides significant orientation, a better jumping-off point is actually the third episode of Season 1, "Chuck vs. the Tango," which presents a textured controlling metaphor that interprets the first three episodes as a whole. However, this image is not the one featured in the episode title, as one might expect. While the dance metaphor mirrors some aspects of the brave new world Chuck encounters in the introductory arc and beyond, the impressionistic work of art used to lure a notorious arms dealer out of hiding, titled "Water Lillies I" (sic), proves the more deeply layered figure. Indeed, the episode should perhaps more appropriately be called "Chuck vs. the Painting."

It is difficult to ignore the landscape canvas. Accented by sinister tones in the soundtrack, the painting fills the dark-filtered screen for the first several moments of the episode. As the camera pans back, the viewer absorbs a seemingly serene pond strewn with blooming lilies and pads floating in clusters. Between them, the still, mirror-like water reflects a combination of inverted trees and clouded sky looming overhead, the sources of which remain hidden from view outside the frame. These phantom reflections of shadow and murky light not only mask the actual surface of the water with a false appearance but render it impossible for the viewer to determine what lurks beneath. The artist (in the general style and theme of Monet's famed series of the same name) further blurs the boundaries between objects on the canvas with layered brush strokes that produce blended colors.

Following this initial foregrounding, the camera lens continues to focus on the painting as it is repeatedly transferred from the possession of one underworld thug to another, but only after each shadowy courier pays the ultimate price. Eventually, it becomes the centerpiece of the auction intended to gain the attention of La Ciudad, the faceless underworld trafficker. But the painting also pointedly draws the attention of Chuck, who unknowingly makes the target's acquaintance while admiring the piece, though Chuck admits to her that his interest lies more with the frame. This strategic and pronounced placement of "Water Lillies" is no coincidence.

Though "vs. the Tango" is only the third installment of the series, Chuck's seemingly serene world, like elements in the painting, has already been turned upside down largely due to forces hidden from his frame of reference. Moreover, his plunge into the murky pond of espionage comes with a pointed difficulty in distinguishing between appearance and reality on multiple levels. In one regard, the introductory arc illustrates these dynamics at the plot level. Chuck not only has no conception of the chain of events that lead to his receiving and downloading the ultra-secret Intersect from Bryce Larkin, his Stanford frenemy, but he thinks Larkin is working as an accountant, not an allegedly dead, rogue spy. Moreover, Chuck finds his life suddenly endangered when he is flipped without notice into an intelligence asset even as the CIA and NSA converge on his formerly tranquil Burbank existence to impose 24/7 surveillance, at least when agents from the respective agencies don't battle each other over him. Further muddying matters, and also hidden outside Chuck's framework, an erstwhile protector, Casey, may transform into his assassin, per Beckman's call at Larkin's funeral, should circumstances change and the new human Intersect prove a liability. For good measure, the treacherous Dr. Zarnow is literally hidden from Chuck during the neurological exam in the same episode, and not without reason as it turns out.

In addition, "Water Lillies" figures Chuck's difficulty seeing below the phantom surface of his new, inverted spy world. On the level of characterization, correctly distinguishing between the good guys and the bad guys certainly does not come naturally to the Nerd Herder. Indeed, Chuck has a hard time making heads and tails of whom to trust, often getting misled by outward appearances. In Episode 2, Chuck alternately and erroneously determines that Casey and Sarah, both now tasked with protecting him, are traitorous enemies due to his limited espionage framework. When not suspecting Casey due to the NSA incinerator found in Zarnow's bombed car, Chuck doubts Sarah's real identity and intentions after he flashes on her prior assassin mission in Europe. The latter 'mistake' ultimately earns him an ironic rebuke from his miffed handler: "I didn't tell you to believe me; I asked you to trust me." Meanwhile, Chuck remains convinced that Bryce Larkin's motives were hostile in getting him kicked out of Stanford and allegedly stealing his girl, unaware that Larkin was actually looking out for him. That insight won't start dawning on Chuck for a few more episodes (vs. the Alma Mater).

Episode 3 repeats this identity confusion while expanding its scope. The La Ciudad mission, his first, comes only after Sarah, notably citing his insufficient training, is overruled by Beckman and Graham, powers again looming beyond Chuck's early espionage horizon. Prior to the mission, Chuck, still a stranger to the lethal nature of the underworld, almost comically wonders aloud about why La Ciudad's victims are sleeping in the photographs he reviews. During the mission, he proceeds to confuse an MI6 agent with La Ciudad (sending Casey and Sarah on a goose chase) before innocently accepting a beautiful guest's invitation to tango, only to discover his dance partner is actually the very villain who will later violently threaten and nearly take his life.

The deeper Chuck is lead into the shadow world as a spy, like the blended brush strokes of "Water Lillies," the more indistinct the boundaries become separating the espionage realm from his normal one. It starts with an interrupted family dinner party that masks his handlers' struggle against each other to control the asset and continues with a private dancing lesson with Awesome in Chuck's living room that doubles as misguided mission prep for Chuck's next 'date.' In the early going, Chuck tries to keep his personal life with Ellie on a separate, transparent plane from the morally murky one on which the spy world operates. Apologizing for his "evasive" answers when discussing his seemingly budding relationship with Sarah, Chuck tells Ellie he doesn't want to lie to her, but by Episode 8 (vs. the Truth) it becomes increasingly difficult to remain honest without divulging his secret life and thus endanger her. Chuck laments the merging of his worlds in an exchange with Sarah after

Dr. Ellie unwittingly becomes entangled with his shadow life by coming to the medical aid of a stranger:

> **Chuck:** I'm getting way too comfortable lying and sneaking around…all this spy stuff, OK. I'm starting to feel like that's my real life.
>
> **Sarah:** It's all to be expected. It's an existential spy crisis of sorts.
>
> **Chuck:** It used to be all compartmentalized, you know: Chuck World and Spy World. But when I saw those ambulance doors close and I saw my sister was behind them with that sweaty nuclear spy freak, my worlds collided.

Meanwhile, the painting's new frame, storing the nuclear material La Ciudad seeks, also implies that Chuck's call to duty as a CIA spy will require him to re-frame his doubt-filled view of himself, a point highlighted when Chuck notes his particular interest in the frame to the arms dealer. Even in regards to his normal life, Ellie tells her Nerd Herd brother, "I…know what an incredible guy Charles Bartowski is, and sometimes I'm not so sure that he knows it" (vs. the Tango). Similarly, Chuck confesses difficulty considering himself a spy let alone a hero when he succeeds in the introductory episodes. At the close of Episode 2, when it becomes apparent that Chuck will be serving as the Intersect indefinitely after Dr. Zarnow's betrayal, Sarah tackles this issue head on, challenging Chuck, "Some people want to be heroes, and others need to be asked….So, Chuck,…are you ready?" In reply, he can only muster an incomplete "Yeah" and a timid nod. At the close of Episode 3, Chuck again needs a pep talk to recognize his achievement even after he has helped to take down a vaunted international criminal:

> **Sarah:** Congratulations on your first mission! You did really good, Chuck.
>
> **Chuck:** Stop it! I'm not really a spy. A computer ended up in the head of a guy who only knows how to fix them, nothing else.
>
> **Sarah:** You survived a near-death experience under the threat

of torture and apprehended one of the world's most elusive killers. I'm not sure what you think spies do, exactly, but most of us would consider that a pretty good day.

Chuck: OK, sure. So today I helped take down a major international arms dealer, but tomorrow, tomorrow I still got to go clock in at Buy More. I mean what's the good of being a hero if nobody knows about it?

Sarah: You know….and so do I.

Sarah's concluding personal comment serves as the perfect link between "Water Lillies" and its equally significant role as a figure for the romantic elements of the introductory arc. In parallel fashion, Chuck finds his personal life turned upside down and suddenly complicated when Sarah enters the frame. Chuck himself testifies to this fact in the first episode of Season 2 (vs. the First Date) when, speaking of Sarah, he asks Ellie, "You know when you meet someone and they kind of flip you on your head?" Already bewildered by the increasingly obscured boundaries of Chuck World and the spy world, he also finds the lines separating his cover and real relationships with his handler growing less distinct as a personal connection seems to emerge with Sarah. Of course, this aspect of his espionage immersion will ultimately prove more light than shadow to Chuck.

Though Sarah will confess in Season 3 that she fell for Chuck during the pilot "sometime between fixing my phone and diffusing a bomb with a virus" (vs. the Other Guy), enough clues lurk within "vs. the Tango" alone, ignoring the flirtation of the first two episodes, to paint their quickly blurring relationship. Early in the episode, Sarah informs Chuck the time has come to "sell" their cover relationship and brazenly instructs the bashful Nerd Herder to kiss her smack in the middle of the Buy More. When this elicits only a tentative peck on the cheek, Sarah seems a tad disappointed at Chuck's aversion to "PDA" ("That's it?"), but she still relishes the opportunity to tease him further by tugging him to a "more private" location, the video room, for briefing. Similar affection crops up at the Wienerlicious while prepping Chuck for his first mission. After Chuck confesses his anxiety over the shadowy events looming before him, as well as answering the increasingly personal questions Sarah asks regarding his painful past with Bryce Larkin, it proves difficult for the viewer to discern whether or not the hand that impulsively reaches out across the table to grasp his is strictly that of a handler assuring her asset.

If these clues do not cloud the asset-handler boundary for him, Chuck certainly decodes Sarah's first overt signal when she verbalizes her feelings about him in the flirtatious scene that closes the episode and serves as a book end to the painting imagery that opens it. As Chuck walks Sarah out following their cover dinner date at Chuck and Ellie's apartment, they pass by the courtyard fountain, which through all five of the series' seasons is pointedly filled with serenely floating lily pads, directly imitating the painting. In some episodes, including the pilot, the lilies have burst into full bloom. Accordingly, Chuck and Sarah's real relationship blossoms as they stand beside the fountain and Chuck ironically notes their cover relationship:

> **Chuck:** You know, if we were really dating, this is the part where I would be forced to kiss you good night.
>
> **Sarah** (smiling): Forced? Would it really be that bad?
>
> **Chuck** (grinning): I'm sure I could suffer through it.
>
> **Sarah** (without pretense, looking into his eyes): Me, too.

Within this context, the words of Chuck's friend and nemesis in Season 2 provide added texture. When dressing with Bryce Larkin for a mission at Sarah's apartment in Episode 3 (vs. the Breakup), Chuck denies that their relationship is anything other than a cover, despite the long-stemmed rose and bottle of wine he showed up with the night before. Unconvinced, Larkin ironically remarks, "I was afraid you'd let the lines get blurred and fall for her." And they certainly do. In fact, Sarah enjoys such a reputation for "falling for every guy that she works with" that in an upcoming episode Casey will ironically inform Sarah he's "not interested, Sister" (vs. the Imported Hard Salami). Sarah herself concedes this point in Season 3, initially telling Shaw, "It's becoming a pattern for me to get involved with guys that I work with, and I really need to put a stop to that before it starts," adding, "I need to stop mixing my personal life with my professional life" (vs. the Fake Name). Given this tendency to obscure relational lines, the impressionist garden paintings decorating Sarah's hotel room serve a figurative as well as decorative purpose.

So, just as with Chuck's existential spy crisis, "Water Lillies" also foreshadows the haziness that will continue to loom over Chuck and Sarah's blossoming relationship. Indeed, the status of their relationship, whether simply a cover or real, will remain indistinct for the bulk of two seasons. Chuck will struggle with whether he can achieve a normal life with Sarah, and Sarah will struggle with how her feelings can coexist within the barriers of both her spy and personal life. The latter of which leads to Chapter 2: Fish Out of Water.

CHAPTER 2:

Fish Out of Water

Right on the heels of one controlling metaphor, another appears soon after the opening of Episode 4 (vs. the Wookiee). While the painting in "vs. the Tango" primarily interprets Chuck's Season 1 plight, a subsequent figure, actually a sequence of events beginning and ending with a goldfish, develops the complexities of Agent Sarah Walker. And she is "complicated." But first the context.

Before Sarah returns to her hotel room for the night, the first few minutes of "vs. the Wookiee" focus on her cover date with Chuck and the rest of the 'family,' including Awesome and Morgan, at his and Ellie's apartment. While chowing down on pizza (in Sarah's case, without olives), they play a spirited rendition of The Newlywed Game, each player trying to guess answers to questions regarding teammates' personal lives. Sarah, seemingly at home while smirking, smiling and even flirting with Chuck, is able to correctly answer a question pertaining to Chuck's childhood dog (even if Morgan protests on a technicality). Chuck, though, finds himself at a total loss (and indisposed) to provide a correct answer regarding Sarah's most dangerous moment. Meanwhile, an indistinct presence lurking outside the open windows and rustling curtains pointedly unsettles Sarah, distracting her from the levity within. Just another spy assignment for Agent Walker, right?

Not really. More typically, Sarah returns to her silent, empty hotel room to shower and prepare for another day of burning cover hot dogs. Remembering to feed her pet goldfish, she kneels down before the transparent bowl, grabs the fish food and gazes upon her solitary counterpart floating within. After a pronounced couple of moments, Sarah stirs herself from her reverie and arises to run the shower water, only to glimpse the masked figure of Carina reflected in the fixtures. Of course, a struggle ensues leaving them out of breath and with at least one bloody nose. Notably, though, the skirmish does not end before the goldfish bowl is upended and the fish sloshes out on to the carpet, floundering for oxygen. Capping an otherwise comic moment, Carina, spotting the poor fish's plight, suspends the fight just long enough to grab it with her gloved hand, throw it back into safety, and right the bowl. Though this figurative sequence may not seem integral to the episode at first glance, deeper scrutiny reveals key elements pertinent to interpreting Sarah for the bulk of the series' first two seasons.

In the first portion of this scene, Sarah's intrigue with the pet initiates her link to a fish motif woven throughout the series. In Season 4 (vs. Phase Three), Morgan will explicitly identify Sarah as "kind of a big fish" when discussing the reasons behind Chuck's delayed engagement proposal. This reference further resonates with imagery found in the Season 1 finale: Lizzie the Pita Palace delivery girl forces Sarah at gunpoint to slide her Big Mike's soon-to-be smashed marlin, notably holding Ellie's ring, just prior to jailing Sarah in the Wienerlicious freezer and Agent Longshore arriving to escort Chuck to a D. C. bunker.

Simultaneous with this link to the goldfish, the camera lens's unique positioning, depicting Sarah's bleary face through the water-filled bowl, not only foregrounds her pensive mood, a marked contrast to her more animated behavior at the dinner party, but suggests a transparent, unmasked glimpse into Sarah's thoughts. Thus, Sarah's focus on the solitary fish implies her own loneliness. Near the end of the "vs. the Wookiee", Chuck asks Sarah's friendly sparring partner, Carina, why spies don't let anyone know who they really are, and she bluntly replies, "Can't. Might have to leave them in five minutes, or shoot them in the head. Trust me, a spy doesn't want you to know anything about them that's real, no matter who you are." However, Sarah's fuzzy and seemingly magnified face, as seen through the bowl, suggests a distorted degree of isolation in comparison to her peers, stemming from an equally distorted childhood.

As the Season 5 episode "vs. the Baby" makes clear, Sarah, just weeks prior to her assignment to Burbank, pursued a life intensely solitary even for a spy. In fact, her former handler Ryker admits he requested Sarah's assignment to him in Hungary because her file "screamed loner," the ideal type, he felt, to keep hidden the morally suspect secret he knew she would discover. And he was right, at least partially. Though Sarah didn't follow the script Ryker wrote for her, she kept the secret of the baby and its location from everyone, including Chuck as both boyfriend and husband. Not coincidentally, at the start of "vs. the Baby" Sarah receives a cell phone message from a mother so marginalized in her life that even the CIA doesn't know she exists: "…I haven't heard from you for a while…Wherever you are…I want you to know that if you ever need a place to come home to, well, you have one." When transferred to Los Angeles, Sarah also pointedly prefers to live in a hotel room, allegedly out of a suitcase, for the better part of three years. Even Casey, not one to put down roots, settles in to an apartment by the third episode of Season 1 and calls his mother on Christmas Eve in Season 2 when Sarah does not (vs. the Santa Claus).

Multiple causes for this hermetic lifestyle surface throughout the series, but the lessons learned under the tutelage of her conman father during her itinerate childhood left perhaps the deepest impression. Checking in and out of hotels on the road became the norm for Sarah, who assumed a new alias in each town they worked. Matters only grew worse with time. When her father reached the end of the road with his arrest, Sarah also faced abandonment. In Season 2 (vs. the Cougars), Chuck tries to comfort Sarah over a pummeled punching bag with the idea that her high school woes were likely typical, but she cryptically confesses, "It was more than that for me." Indeed, flashbacks reveal her teenage years as the period when her father was imprisoned and, to survive, Sarah surrendered herself to the loving arms of the CIA. Transience and abandonment only raised the height of her emotional walls. In Season 4's "vs. the Wedding Planner," Sarah's father admits he coached Sarah "to keep things close" as a child, adding, "The second you let your guard down, you get hurt." Sarah confirms this in "vs. the Baby". "…It's what my dad taught me. It's the way the CIA taught me: that you can ever only trust yourself." No wonder Sarah confides to Chuck in the pilot over dinner, "…I may come with some baggage," a warning that extends beyond her recent past with Bryce Larkin.

However, Sarah's "complicated" character evidences an additional, more subtle dimension as well. In opposition to her distorted childhood and current spy life, in which she feels safe if isolated, Sarah also nurses closely guarded thoughts that invest her with an ironic dual nature. Deep down, Sarah clings to the latent dream of family and a normal life in the future, starting even prior to Season 1. Her last words to her mother in "vs. the Baby" reveal she has considered similar issues in recent weeks or months. When her mother laments the "normal life" of trick-or-treating and soccer games that Sarah missed, Sarah tearfully replies, "...All those normal things that you wanted for me: will you make sure that [Molly] gets them?" Later in Season 1 (vs. the Crown Vic), the topic still occupies Sarah's mind when she asks Casey, "Do you ever just want to have a normal life? Have a family? Children?" By Season 5 (vs. the Zoom), Sarah even reveals she has envisioned a dream house since childhood, complete with a picket fence.

Early on in the series, Sarah's future dream subtly links itself to Chuck, in whom she finds the vaguest prospect of attaining these normal ideals. Sarah's question to Casey about a normal life, family and children is pointedly asked in the midst of a conversation over whether Sarah, while under the truth serum, compromised herself with the asset who awkwardly offered to serve as her "very own baggage handler" on their first 'date.' By Sarah's own admission, the unassuming, verbal, funny, and sweet Nerd Herder began slipping behind her emotional barriers as early as the pilot when helping fix her cell phone and saving one very disappointed ballerina (vs. the Other Guy). Three years later, Sarah makes another crucial revelation. After Chuck discovers the picture of Sarah and him taken in Season 2 during the Montgomery mission lodged in her suitcase, Sarah confesses it makes her feel "safe" whether in L.A. or on the road, adding, "You're my home....You always have been" (vs. the Suitcase). This sheds added light on Sarah's private exchange with Carina after the goldfish scene in "vs. the Wookiee." Whereas her globe-trotting C.A.T. pal describes Burbank as "If a yawn could yawn," Sarah replies firmly, "I'm good here," an affirmation of her new hometown that indicates just how different the two spies have become.

These conflicting elements of Sarah's dual nature, the dominant isolated spy element and the latent dream of family and a normal life potentially linked to Chuck, are figured immediately after Sarah leaves the solitary goldfish for the bathroom. As she turns on the shower and reaches her hand to check the flow, the camera lens notably captures the distinct reflection of Sarah's face in the tiling, presenting the actual (i.e. solitary spy life) and the phantom (i.e. dream of normal life) images side by side in the frame. Given this figuring, the scene also signifies a potential baptism: Sarah tests the stream with her hand to determine whether it's time to enter and immerse herself in the waters of change even as she contemplates the possibility of a transition from one life to the other. Before she can proceed, however, a masked intruder appears in the fixture. Entering the shower will have to wait.

Of course, Carina ends up pulling off the mask, but exactly what unwelcome prowler does she personify when waylaying Sarah before she can step into a new life? It is the same indistinct presence that lurks outside Chuck's apartment on game night, unsettling Sarah and preventing her from fully enjoying her blossoming relationship with Chuck and his 'family.' Simply put, the tenacious intruder is her fear of the unknown. While Sarah's goldfish existence may increasingly expose its defects, it is emotionally safe, and Sarah knows how to float behind its walls. Making the leap to an alternative world will prove risky and extremely problematic.

In one regard, the professional boundary the CIA expects a handler and an asset to observe, and which Sarah feels compelled to honor, proves a barrier in her ability to pursue a romantic relationship with Chuck. As the assignment of a 49B makes clear in Season 2 (vs. the Broken Heart), the loss of her assignment and its negative effect on her career is a real possibility, especially given the increased surveillance as the series progresses. And if Sarah is prevented from naturally pursuing the relationship, how can she be assured that what she feels is real and not an artificial byproduct of her handling role? Will she feel the same way when the CIA completes another Intersect and she is free to leave? And how will a relationship with Chuck work with her next assignment? This is to say nothing of Sarah's anxiety over how she can fit into the normal world, in which she has enjoyed no experience or mentors. Remember, this is a woman who will display significant qualms over unpacking a suitcase and prefer a knife fight in Peru over planning an engagement party.

The metaphorical melee between Sarah and Carina that diverts her from the baptismal shower is a violent affair. Notably, it upends the goldfish bowl, signifying the degree to which the dueling elements of Sarah's nature, ironically exacerbated by her emerging feelings for Chuck and fear of the unknown, has upended her life even as soon as Episode 4. Amidst the rough and tumble, Sarah's nose is bloodied, even though she claims Carina "telegraph[s]" her punches. Similarly, Sarah's fear will periodically inhibit her pursuit of Chuck, even though she can see its fists coming. The fight ends with Carina (i.e. her fears) returning the fish to the security of the fishbowl, recalling Sarah's inability to step into the shower and further suggesting she isn't quite ready to leave the safety of the familiar in Season 1, despite its drawbacks. Beforehand, though, the creature notably flounders for oxygen, implying the emotional struggle Sarah will experience for much of the first two seasons as she is increasingly drawn out from her isolated spy life and into the rarified air of Chuck's normal world.

And struggle she does. A relationship with Chuck will ultimately require at least a minimal level of trust and transparency, and she doesn't get very far before stumbling on that score. Even before leaving the courtyard following the game night she finds herself misleading an inquisitive Chuck. In her own awkward attempt to minimize her isolation and foster some level of transparency, Sarah informs Chuck he can "always ask" questions to satisfy his curiosity about her. Unfortunately, the first question turns out to be an uncomfortable one regarding the nature of her prior relationship with Bryce Larkin. Her less-than-forthcoming response later shakes Chuck's trust ("I thought you were supposed to be good at lying") when he learns the truth from the always conniving Carina and leaves a visibly disconcerted Sarah staring blankly into space after he storms out of the Wienerlicious. Moreover, Chuck's hurt feelings directly affect his behavior on the subsequent mission to recover the diamond, endangering it and causing a headache for his handler.

In a bookend, Sarah's struggle with transparency resurfaces at her hotel room in the concluding scene of "vs. the Wookiee." The video log report pertaining to this scene, found in Season 5's "vs. Sarah," notes that Chuck brought a pizza, "vegetarian, no olives," before Sarah comments, "I think he's making it his mission to get to know me." For the short term, at least, that looks like Mission Impossible. After making his peace with Sarah's past with Bryce Larkin, Chuck confesses, "I just wish I knew something real about you," adding, "Can't you just tell me one true thing?" When asked where she grew up or her real name, Sarah proves so conflicted that she is capable of, again, merely staring ahead glassy-eyed and silent. Only when Chuck leaves to grab some napkins, out of earshot, does she manage the courage to whisper the answer to his last, seemingly minor request: her middle name.

The fish-out-of-water metaphor also foreshadows Sarah's internal skirmish when it comes to admitting her developing feelings for Chuck, despite plentiful evidence to the contrary. Ellie is the first to notice, telling a doubtful Chuck, "Ah, trust me. I have seen the way that girl looks at you, and she is into you" (vs. the Tango). Carina knows Sarah better than anyone in Burbank, and before she leaves at the end of "vs. the Wookiee" she admits to Chuck that she tried to seduce him because she loves "taking what Sarah wants." When Chuck again voices his skepticism, Carina voices her certainty: "She probably doesn't even know it herself yet, but I do." Casey consistently echoes Carina's view throughout the first two seasons, starting with his question to Sarah about whether she compromised herself with the asset while under the influence of the truth serum (vs. the Truth). Sarah's reply speaks volumes: "No….If I had not been trained to withstand Pentothal, I might have." The most vivid piece of evidence, of course, proves Sarah's passionate kissing of Chuck when she thinks their lives are about to abruptly end in the next episode (vs. the Imported Hard Salami).

Despite the multiple objective verifications and her own explicit behavior, Sarah still flip-flops, alternately deluding herself and denying her genuine feelings for Chuck. Sarah's reaction to the impulsive act of kissing Chuck seems to confirm Carina's prior assessment about her lack of self-awareness. When recording her video log response to the event (vs. Sarah), Sarah's repetition of "I kissed him," combined with her shaking head, rolling eyes, and sigh, suggests that she still can't really wrap her mind around the fact. Eventually, she will insist on referring to the kiss as "The Incident" to downplay its import and call it "a mistake, one that I will not make again" (vs. the Crown Vic). According to the video log, it will take until the latter half of Season 2 for Sarah to admit her love for Chuck even to herself, let alone anyone else. In some cases, Sarah's self-delusion verges on the comical. In "vs. the Imported Hard Salami," a single day before she feels compelled to kiss him, Sarah misleads Chuck and perhaps herself, saying, "Look, I'm sorry if you thought there was something between us. It's very common in these situations to perceive a connection that isn't there." In the same episode, Sarah insists, "I haven't fallen for Chuck," to which Casey can only laugh, "Whatever you say!"

The conflict between Sarah's alienated past and private dream of a normal future extends all the way to the final scene of Season 1 (vs. the Marlin). In an image that reiterates the fishbowl sequence presented in "vs. the Wookiee," though using a different framework, Sarah and Chuck stand outside the window of his and Ellie's apartment having just avoided Chuck's bunkering in D.C. or capture by Fulcrum with the narrowest of margins. Drawn to the symbolic initiation of a family, an initially smirking Sarah urges Chuck to join her in spying on Awesome's engagement proposal. Chuck, standing in front, notes Ellie's joy while Sarah, in agreement, pointedly observes from a more distant vantage point over his shoulder.

The camera, positioned to display their faces through the glass, recalls that of the fish bowl scene, with the viewer again provided a transparent view into Sarah's thoughts. While Chuck doesn't take his eyes off his sister and soon-to-be brother-in-law, Sarah's quickly-glazing eyes notably dart back and forth between Chuck and the couple inside even while she repeatedly swallows back emotion. When Chuck muses, "I couldn't leave them yet," Sarah, her smirk replaced by thin, pursed lips, assures him, "You don't have to worry about that. You're safe." Doubtless, Sarah desires to protect Chuck for his sake, his family's sake, and the nation's sake, and she will certainly do whatever it takes to stand between him and the shadowy forces threatening him outside the window frame. It is a mistake, however, to miss the more subtle but pressing force behind her angst: her unspoken desire to keep her personal intersection with the normal world secure. Indeed, her words apply as much to herself as they do to Chuck. This aspect actually foreshadows the thinking behind Sarah's crucial decision in "vs. the Santa Claus" in Season 2 (See Chapter 7: Thunder and Rain).

But when Chuck invites her to join him inside, Sarah declines, citing it a "family" time. Though Chuck tellingly replies, "I know," Sarah, after pausing, elects to keep her emotions hidden and instead bids him good night. Sarah is simply not yet prepared to accept such a symbolic gesture in Season 1. Still, after Chuck enters the apartment, Sarah can't help but linger outside the window, an intrigued spectator of normal life, her face betraying a forlorn expression contrasting vividly with the family celebration within. Casey suddenly appears behind her, posing as a variation of Sarah's prowling fear, to deliver another harrowing punch: "We can only keep him here for so long. You realize that, don't you?" As Sarah envisions the full impact of that prospect, the ominous crescendo of the soundtrack confirms Sarah's internal floundering. A floundering that leaves her once again staring with glassy eyes, set jaw, and pursed lips, looking every bit a fish out of water.

CHAPTER 3:

Woman on Top?

Sarah: I need you to do one more thing for me.

Chuck: Yeah?

Sarah: Trust me, Chuck.

With these words, spoken on a Malibu beach in the pilot, Chuck surrenders to the protection of Agent Sarah Walker. Truth be known, his handler has already taken the driver's seat, implied by her positioning to Chuck's left on the sand. Somewhere in the middle of their cover date the night before, when Casey and a team of NSA agents closed in on Chuck and his CIA "skirt," Sarah demanded the keys to the Nerd Herd vehicle. When Chuck took too long to comply, she simply inserted her own magical high-tech substitute and started the car herself while commanding him to "get in!" Within moments Sarah was performing driving gymnastics in reverse, and she will continue to serve as Chuck's chauffeur for the first several episodes of Season 1, though in her much more stylish Porsche. At the outset of the series, Chuck is just coming along for the very harrowing ride.

Chuck's submission further evidences itself in the questions he asks Agent Walker before they leave the beach: "What are you going to do with me? What happens now?" Accordingly, Sarah begins to lay down the rules of the road: go home, tell no one in order to protect them, and work with us until further notice. She also assumes the role of espionage mentor, teaching Chuck such basic lessons as observing the proper tailing distance, avoiding talk of being a spy on missions, and—most importantly--staying in the car. However, when Chuck's trust falters in Episode 2 (vs. the Helicopter) and he briefly takes the wheel (or is that the landing stick?), he receives a harsh rebuke from his handler, who even threatens him with the prospect of a Washington, D.C., bunker. The second-guessing comes to an abrupt stop.

When Chuck also submits to Sarah's cover dating scheme, her control begins to extend beyond the spy world and enters into their emerging not-so-fake relationship as well. This new dynamic is figured elsewhere in Season 1 through a pair of comical metaphors. In one indirect image, the Intersect, thanks to Awesome, learns the woman's part of the tango, highlighting his passive role as both asset and cover boyfriend (vs. the Tango). If it's any comfort, Chuck has company. A symmetrical reference inserted into Season 2 pointedly shows an authoritative Sarah rejecting Bryce's plea to let him lead their salacious cover tango at Von Hayes' party (vs. the Break-Up).

However, the most vivid figuring of the initial romantic power dynamic between Chuck and Sarah pops up in Episode 8 of Season 1 (vs. the Truth), which opens with the head Nerd Herder and his handler conducting an unorthodox briefing while locked in the Wienerlicious closet. With mock anxiety, they rehearse the details of their cover date with Ellie and Awesome only to hear Sarah's boss approach the door. Instinctively, her Wienerliciousness further unbuttons the top of her uniform, forces Chuck to the floor and straddles him. And just in the nick of time. When the door opens, Sarah slowly removes her lips from Chuck's neck, in no hurry to dismount, and meets Scooter's gaze with a look more coy than sheepish. The manager with the unfortunate hairstyle and voice to match proceeds to utter perhaps his only meaningful words in the series: "Wow! Girl on top," adding an admonition to work instead of playing with her "boy toy." Sarah is clearly in charge of matters, both spy-related and not.

Her control in the latter category starts cutely enough. Sarah makes Chuck blush at the Buy More when sweetly ordering him to sell their cover with a public kiss; all he can muster is a meek peck on the cheek (vs. the Tango). Observing the cuddly manner of Ellie and Awesome on their cover date, Sarah next snuggles up to Chuck with non-verbal cues for him to amp up the PDA (vs. the Truth). Soon, Chuck inquires about the party line on how to respond when asked why they aren't sleeping together after several dates; and after Sarah decides the explanation she dictates ("taking it slow") is growing thin, she deems it "time to make love" and arranges to stay the night in Chuck's room. Sarah even ends a sentence for Chuck when he stalls on describing to his new interest, Lou, the exact nature of his relationship with Sarah: "girlfriend." However, the power dynamic of their 'fake' relationship doesn't remain cute for long, at least not to Chuck.

Chuck actually begins to feel a bit foolish the evening Sarah spends the night in "vs. the Truth." After embarrassing the obviously hopeful Chuck with the question, "What did you think was going to happen here tonight?" Sarah disrobes to model lingerie before slipping into bed, acting as if nothing is out of the ordinary and alleging its necessity for the sake of the cover. Chuck, weary of Sarah yanking his chain with impunity, ultimately seems to forsake his own bed for the floor amidst the surveillance chatter. Before he does so, however, he asks an important question: "What exactly are the rules with our...like, you know...our thing?...Are we allowed to see other people?" Of course Sarah discourages the idea, citing tactical challenges and his strategic value. Though Chuck already entertains the idea of a return to normal life through the pursuit of a real relationship with Lou, the following day's events embolden his resolve. Convinced that Sarah is unable to lie under the influence of the truth serum, he gracefully accepts the news that they have no future together and immediately begins the process of scooting out from beneath her control on this front.

Chuck proves persistent in his little rebellion. If forsaking his own bed the night before was the opening skirmish, he ambushes Sarah the next day. Tenderly holding her arms and looking into her eyes, he voices his desire to "fake break-up our pretend relationship" (vs. the Truth). In a moment of clarity, Chuck, without guile, continues, "...The longer we keep trying to fool people into believing that we're a real couple...the person I keep fooling the most is me." Chuck leaves a speechless Sarah for Lou's sandwich shop and starts getting on with a real life. In "vs. the Imported Hard Salami," Chuck resists Sarah's subsequent attempt to slide back on top. Despite her reasoning that the cover relationship should continue because "it makes things easier," the Intersect firmly responds, "...I guess your job's gonna be a little harder."

And no doubt about it, Sarah is thrown over. Compelled to follow him outside after the initial break-up, she spies Chuck and Lou engaged in animated conversation through the window of the sandwich shop and senses the ground shifting beneath her. Even the jaded, amnesiac version of Sarah at the end of Season 5 can't help but raise her eyebrows when observing the visibly unsettled Sarah of Season 1 disjointedly report that Chuck "broke up with me, well, fake broke up with me, technically" in her video log (vs. Sarah). Agent Walker tells Chuck they'll have to sell the break-up publicly if he insists on going through with it, and, curiously, her sudden performance proves so convincing that even Chuck has a hard time distinguishing it from reality (vs. the Imported Hard Salami). In a striking about-face, Sarah is soon found selling a radically repackaged scenario to Beckman to explain the break-up at the next briefing. When asked, "What the hell happened?" an uncomfortable Sarah replies, "We decided that it would be best for Chuck to date a civilian. It will help secure his cover in the event that someone I.D.'s me." Casey, not buying the pitch, edits it in typically blunt fashion: "…She got dumped!"

And the beat goes on. Likely using Chuck's endangerment as a pretext, Sarah proceeds to exit the van during his date-turned-mission with Lou and ends up, at least in Chuck's mind, sabotaging the evening to the point she feels she must apologize for it the next day. Of course, Sarah's most pronounced loss of control comes later that same day. Uncharacteristically, Sarah loses focus during the mission at the docks when she ends up locked in the car trunk with Chuck. Instead of devising her next move, she engages in an argument that bears the earmarks of a lover's quarrel. With her jaw clenched, Sarah resembles a fish floundering for oxygen when yelling, "You're sucking up all the air! Shut up!" Before the episode ends, Chuck continues to resist Sarah's control when refusing his handler's orders to leave her alone with the bomb, curiously at pistol point, and earning himself a weak rebuke: "Why are you so stubborn?" Standing his ground, Chuck answers, "I guess you just bring out the worst in me," to which Sarah, after glaring and aggressively stepping forward, replies, "And you in me."

Imminent death is perhaps the most powerful force of clarification. Thinking the professional barriers already obsolete as only seconds remain, Sarah initiates The Incident, tacitly admitting the vulnerability of her emotional walls and permanently altering the power dynamic of their relationship. Certainly, Chuck and Sarah both will assume the lead at various times, but from this point forward their bewildering tango will be far more evenly choreographed and executed. Sarah will not always be the girl on top, and Chuck will have his turns at the wheel.

CHAPTER 4:

A Slow and Painful Awakening

The return of Bryce Larkin in Episode 10 (vs. the Nemesis) and the fall-out from Sarah's decision to remain in Burbank in the wake of his departure in Episode 11 (vs. the Crown Vic) collectively pose the first serious threat to Chuck and Sarah's relationship. In reading these potentially ambiguous episodes, the viewer is well-served to recall Sarah's masked internal conflict discussed in Chapter 2: Fish Out of Water. Sarah's choice is not one purely between the suave, courageous and handsome Mr. Anderson and the occasionally awkward, girly, and gangly computer technician. Since Sarah struggles between two factions within her own mind, the isolated, nomadic loner element and her emerging dream of a normal life that offers emotional safety, family and a permanent home, the choice between Bryce and Chuck holds the added dimension of a decision between her problematic past and potential future. Bryce's coded invitation to join up with him for his ultra-secret, itinerant mission simply brings Sarah's inner tension to a climax.

Sarah's wedding vows in Season 4 provide additional context for this decision in Season 1. Three years later, Sarah will regard Chuck as "a gift I never dreamed I could want or need" (vs. the Cliffhanger). Therefore, somewhere along the way Sarah awakens to her deeper desires and needs, and reprioritizes her life to fulfill them. This perspective helps interpret Sarah's interaction with Bryce not only in "vs. the Nemesis" but also in Season 2 (see Chapter 6: Sand Wall). Moreover, it indicates that the decision she makes in her hotel room at episode's end is a critical moment in her private emotional journey. However, no one said this process would quick or easy.

From the first frame of the decisive scene closing "vs. the Nemesis," the camera presents a clearly conflicted Sarah. Most obvious, she is packed and dressed waiting for a phone call from Bryce, her passport prominently displayed on the bed. Surely she has reached her decision, and all that is needed is the unknown location of their rendezvous. Not so fast. Her face pensive, Sarah pointedly stands at the opposite end of the room from the phone that will bring the news. No hovering around the receiver. No hint of enthusiasm in her expression. As she stands, she stares out over the lights of the Los Angeles skyline, her eyes locked on "the only place that felt like home," even though she has "lived all over the world" (vs. the Honeymooners). Significantly, the camera pans upward, starting at Sarah's hands. Her watch, notably reflected in the window, signifies the time has come to choose. Similarly, as the lens rises it reveals the faint but distinct reflection of Sarah's face opposite her actual face, recalling the shower scene in "vs. the Wookiee" by imaging the two factions of her psyche struggling with one another even before the phone rings. When it does, Sarah greets it with a more strained expression, and there is no rush to answer; just the opposite, Sarah does not take a single step toward the phone until (apparently) the fourth ring.

The wistful, dramatic song accenting this montage scene, "No One's Gonna Love You" by Band of Horses, offers further clarity. The words accompanying the close-ups of both Sarah at the hotel window and a distracted, silently distraught Chuck at his apartment mirror their inner turmoil: "If things start splitting at the seams and now / The whole thing's tumbling down / …Hard." When the lens next shifts to Bryce's face for a few moments, the lyrics precisely identify him as "the ever-living ghost of what once was," but when the focus shifts to Chuck's picture on Sarah's phone and then back to Chuck, his ear to his own phone in the apartment, the song repeats, "…No one is ever gonna love you more than I do / No one's gonna love you more than I do." Finally, the lens swings back to the face of Sarah, whose eyes leave the cell phone screen, stare blankly forward, look once towards the ringing phone, and then back to the vibrating phone in her hand. All the while, the refrain repeats: "But someone / They should have warned you / But things start splitting at the seams and now / The whole thing's tumbling down / Hard." When Sarah finally looks up and stares blankly forward one last time, swallowing hard with tears in her eyes, she appears to have made a painful if passive decision. By answering neither phone, she chooses, perhaps even subconsciously, not just Chuck but also a potential normal future with someone in whom she will eventually find a home for her heart instead of continuing on the ever-winding path of her itinerate past.

The morning-after scene, recorded near the beginning of Episode 11 (vs. Crown Vic), figures just how slow and painful Sarah's awakening to all of this will be. Uncharacteristically, she sleeps in late, her dress from the night before still beside her on the bed. Though still groggy after the alarm sounds at 9:30 AM, she snatches the rather large knife she keeps as a teddy bear beneath her pillow and scores a bull's eye on the clock across the room, possibly further hinting at the role of her own biological clock in her decision given comments in "vs. Phase Three" (see Chapter 14). After silencing it, Sarah pulls the sheets over her head and seeks the escape of sleep once more. Indeed, she will arrive for the briefing in Casey's apartment, to a relieved Chuck, only after it has begun. Of particular note, Sarah wears sleeping blinds in the bed scene, the only time in the series they ever appear. This detail further suggests that Sarah remains, at least temporarily, blind to the full depth of her feelings and significance of her decision.

This framework helps make sense of the otherwise incoherent sequence of events that follows. When Sarah does arrive at the briefing, her behavior towards Chuck, who she has apparently just chosen over Bryce, is by no means affectionate. She turns to leave the briefing without saying a word to him, and when Chuck stops her in the courtyard on her way out, her response to his rambling attempt to say he's glad she stayed is a cool pronouncement: "I have a job to do." Chuck later tries to make light of the knifed clock as he meets Sarah in her room for the Lon Kirk mission, joking, "Not a morning person I see." But Sarah offers another cool response: "Well, it depends on the morning." After reviewing their cover in a perfunctory manner, Chuck further attempts to set an upbeat tone for the mission, suggesting it should be fun. Sarah's response? "It's work." Chuck's expression falls, and Sarah, sensing his hurt, seems to rethink her words. But offended, Chuck stops her gesture of fixing his tie, leading Sarah to repeat, "OK. Well a…ready to go to work?" All this from a woman who just two episodes prior, in the midst of the Lou interlude,

22

told Chuck, "If it's any consolation, I never felt our time together was work" (vs. the Imported Hard Salami).

Matters grow worse before they get better. Chuck's naïve jealousy jeopardizes the Lon Kirk mission, and circumstances make Chuck's flash appear inaccurate (vs. the Crown Vic). Dropping in at Chuck's apartment, Sarah ironically confronts the Intersect in front of the Christmas tree. Blind to the truth of her own condition, Sarah accuses Chuck of faking his flash because he let his "emotions get in the way," adding that "things have been a little off since The Incident." Sarah even shouts at Chuck to stop calling the kiss a kiss! After his double take, Chuck attempts to take her blinders off. First, he notes exactly who was responsible for the kiss, and then asks a question that makes Sarah, as she admitted at the time of The Incident, confront the "uncomfortable" truth: "Did you kiss me that night because you thought we were going to die and mine were the most convenient lips around, or was it actually about me?" Unable to admit even to herself the deeper feelings and thoughts she harbors, let alone to Chuck, Sarah, after a wide-eyed pause, answers with an evasion before storming out: "It was a mistake, one that I will not make again."

Why this seemingly incongruent sequence of events after the climactic decision two nights before? Together, they constitute the emotional thrashings of a fish out of water. In uncharted territory with her insuppressible feelings for Chuck, Sarah is vexed over her inexplicable loss of internal control and subsequent confusion, as the video log recorded during Season 2 reveals, over "what to do about it" (vs. Sarah). The woman who can withstand a hail of bullets without flinching is reduced to a frightened stranger in a strange land of new feelings.

Chuck and Sarah hit the reset button before the episode closes. Whereas Chuck's attempt to make Sarah confront the truth failed, Casey's succeeds. Giving Sarah one last chance to "come clean" about compromising herself with the Intersect in the wake of their reprimand from Beckman and Graham over the Lon Kirk fiasco, Sarah again evades answering the question directly, but her response reveals the beginning of Sarah's awakening process nonetheless: "Do you….ever just want to have a normal life? Have a family? Children?" Recognizing the difficulties her genuine feelings have caused, compounded by both Chuck's and her recent behavior, Sarah, after another long and pursed-lip pause, leaves

Casey with a promise: "I'll talk to Chuck. If I can't fix this, then I'm going to ask for a reassignment."

Thankfully, it is fixable. But rather than calling a summit meeting, Sarah and Chuck diffuse the situation naturally. When Casey rebuffs Chuck's photo evidence about the location of the plates, Sarah chooses to trust Chuck despite her earlier suspicions of his flash faking. Not only does Chuck turn out to be right, he heroically saves the boat holding Morgan and Anna by redirecting a guided missile. Likewise, Chuck and Sarah redirect the trajectory of their relationship before it combusts.

Pleasantly surprising Chuck, Sarah shows up to the Buy More Christmas/Holiday party and accepts a new, functional clock from Chuck to replace her ruined one, at the very least foreshadowing their resolve to pursue a more functional relationship over time through honesty. Reprising the accusatory scene in front of the Christmas tree in Chuck's apartment, they stand before the Buy More Christmas tree and confess their common frailty. Most pointedly, Sarah admits, "…As you can see with everything that happened with Bryce, I'm not so good at relationships." After telling her, "That makes two of us," Chuck declines Jeff's offer of the mistletoe, instead extending an olive branch in the form of a friendly handshake and invitation to dance. When Sarah accepts both with a smile, the viewer knows the worst has been avoided, and the best is likely yet to come.

Still, Sarah's awakening is not complete, and it will not always be a pleasant process as it unfolds. In the last episode of the season (vs. the Marlin), it takes another crisis to expose the cold reality of what life without Chuck will be like. When Chuck is hustled prematurely and without notice by Beckman and Graham to an extraction point, bound for a D. C. bunker to secure him from Fulcrum's clutches, Sarah quickly realizes just how frigid her Chuck-less world will be, both literally and figuratively. Subdued by Lizzie, the Pita Palace delivery girl and Fulcrum agent, Sarah is pointedly jailed in the Wienerlicious refrigerator room even as Chuck is en route to the helipad with Agent Longshore. By the time Casey releases a nearly frozen Agent Walker and, sensing her angst, graciously sends Sarah to pursue Chuck, it appears to be too late. With Chuck's cover likely blown due to the Pita girl still at large, what reason could prevent Chuck's departure even if she reaches him before the chopper lands?

By the time she arrives at the helipad, minutes from the end of a relationship with Chuck as she has known it, a suddenly desperate Sarah notably grips her pistol while stammering in her attempt to convince Longshore to grant a minute's delay for at least parting words with "my guy." When she finally faces him, all pretenses vanish: unashamed, Sarah allows the tears to fill her eyes and finally spill down her cheek, grasping Chuck's hands even as she begins to grasp the depth of her feelings for him. Only Chuck's poignant humor can briefly turn her pained grimace into a smile. By the time Lizzie arrives to shoot Longshore and grant Chuck and Sarah a new lease on their relationship, Sarah has already assured Chuck not "see you later" but "save you later."

The emotional distance Sarah covers in the last few episodes of Season 1 is dramatic. Within that span, Sarah migrates from calling her kiss of Chuck "a mistake" and considering a reassignment to finding herself on the cusp of accepting a real date with a "fantastic" guy in the Season 2 debut (vs. the First Date). Still, Season 2 will bring additional revelations to Sarah as she continues to fully awaken to her latent dreams and genuine feelings for Chuck. And each time a crisis will further jolt her out of her slumber.

CHAPTER 5:

Symmetries & Ironies

For a show thematically obsessed with differences between appearance and reality, it should surprise no one to find "Chuck" saturated with a motif of ironic inversion. Perhaps no stretch of the dramedy evidences a higher concentration of such incongruities than the first several episodes of Season 2, oftentimes developed within a variety of parallels.

One central plot element, Chuck's potential discharge from the CIA if the new Intersect comes online, is thickly layered with inversions (vs. the First Date). Chuck risks his life to secure the Cypher, a device enabling the completion of the new Intersect project, not once but twice; however, doing so requires his subsequent elimination as an obsolete intelligence liability. Indeed, the reward Graham decrees for Chuck's heroic service is not his release back to a normal life but an execution "with honor" at the hands of Casey. Thinking his CIA discharge near, Chuck proceeds to thank his potential assassin for past help, but when the Cypher is stolen back and Chuck confides his angst over the delay in realizing his bright future, Casey warns, "The future's a dangerous thing. It doesn't always work out like you want it to."

In fact, the same agent who repeatedly tells Chuck he wants a new assignment away from the Buy More to become a real spy again suddenly proves in no hurry to pursue the Cypher and receive a transfer given what it entails. Usually "unquestioning of [his] orders" (vs. Sarah), the super sniper even pitches his superiors on an alternative to killing Chuck before missing the target of Chuck from close range. When Casey does ultimately stalk Chuck per orders, he does so only after already having saved Chuck's life twice in the same episode. And

Graham's eventual come-uppance for the order? His own death in an Intersect white room explosion.

Alternatively, "vs. the First Date" sets up the framework for a subsequent ironic inversion central to Chuck and Sarah's very real cover relationship in Season 2. When Chuck manages to get his hands on the Cypher for the new Intersect, the high-tech acquisition not only promises Chuck an imminent return to normal life by enabling a rebuilt Intersect, but, as the name metaphorically suggests, the key to decoding Sarah's real feelings when potential ulterior motives stemming from her handler role are removed. Events in this episode dispel any lingering doubts on this score.

Though Sarah initially claims "a hundred reasons" why she shouldn't accept Chuck's date while still a CIA agent, she takes the risk and shows visible interest in the prospect. When Chuck calls her bluff, she doesn't fold. While Chuck rattles off Sarah's qualities over dinner, her suddenly vulnerable expression is notable, and when Chuck sarcastically describes himself as "fantastic," Sarah firmly corrects, "Yeah, you are." The only barrier to completing the all-too-mutual kiss after Sarah betrays regret over her likely transfer is Chuck's ill-timed flash. No problem: when the first date dissolves into another mission, Sarah accepts a second date. Except this time there is a problem: when the Intersect upload goes awry, Chuck remains the Intersect, and Sarah must cancel the date. No wonder Chuck told Ellie he and Sarah would be "hitting The Echo" after dinner; suddenly the status of their relationship is right back where they started, right?

Not quite. Though they find themselves returned to the invisible prison of handler-asset protocol, Chuck now enjoys the certainty that he's not just being taken for an emotional ride. This clarification frames a key element of their ironically inverted romance: Chuck and Sarah can act out their real, private passion for one another only when engaged in a fake, public relationship. Whereas they do not kiss on their only real date, Chuck and Sarah share a pair of sizzling kisses while at work in "vs. the Seduction" alone. The first occurs after the cart-wheeling lioness prowls her way up to the Nerd Herd desk to the strains of Huey Lewis' "Do You Believe in Love?" and pulls Chuck to her lips by the tie before yanking him off by the hand to a national emergency. Who needs a real date? Moreover, from Chuck's pleased but nonchalant response, it seems likely the outwardly effervescent slo-mo footage actually presents Sarah's usually guarded inward perspective.

Chuck and Sarah release their collective private passion a second time under the experienced eye of none other than Agent Roan Montgomery. Though Chuck demurs as long as possible, the goading ridicule of Montgomery, Sarah's unsolicited support and permission, and -- most comical -- Montgomery's threat to call in Casey to demonstrate in Chuck's place compel the Intersect to demonstrate his skill. Grabbing Agent Walker by the arm, he yanks her toward him and embraces Sarah, who, though taken by surprise, quickly recovers to reach for his face and extend the kiss into a spicy affair. The viewer gets the feeling that Chuck and Sarah have forgotten all about Montgomery until the kiss ends as suddenly as it began. Taken aback, their 'mentor' can only quietly comment "Bravo!" when they finally separate, and Sarah needs the hurried excuse of fixing her lipstick to settle herself.

However, Sarah also finds more subtle ways to code her feelings for Chuck in public and private. Indeed, these carefully guarded, muted expressions of romantic longing demonstrate additional irony by com-municating her passion just as or more deeply than more pronounced, public expressions on normal dates. No gesture in the series associates itself with Sarah's authentic longing for her private asset more than the simple gesture of silently caressing his neck with her thumb while staring into his eyes. Interestingly, the first occasion of this gesture, when Sarah caresses Chuck on the double date in front of Morgan and Carina (vs. the Wookiee), likely provides a clue to Sarah's gal pal, who later tells Chuck that Sarah really is into him. The second instance occurs in "vs. the Seduction" after Chuck's rescue of Sarah from the Black Widow outside the Buy More via a rooftop banner. While Chuck still lay on the ground, Sarah rushes over to him, her tied hands pointedly figuring their imposed professional restraints, and holds his face before stroking his neck with one hand and placing another over his heart.

In the scenes perhaps most brimming with unfulfilled passion, Sarah reaches out for Chuck's neck in the closing moments of the 'break-up' in the next episode (vs. the Break-Up), and again when standing outside the mobile home of Chuck's dad (vs. the Broken Heart), a time when she is metaphorically cuffed by General Beckman's hope not to see Agent Forrest again soon in the wake of the 49B interval. In a separate muted display of affection, Chuck and Sarah each treasure a cuddly picture of themselves, taken during the Montgomery mission in Episode 2, in their respective homes. Sarah's copy, ironically, first appears on the counter before her bedroom mirror in the episode immediately following their break-up (vs. the Cougars).

This leads to a third major set of ironic inversions surrounding the 'break-up' in "vs. the Break-Up," though the event is more appropriately termed the 'non-break-up.' In one regard, it proves ironically symmetrical to the first break-up in Season 1 (vs. the Truth). Both events are triggered by the same alleged reason, but Chuck and Sarah switch roles in triggering them: in Season 1, Chuck elects to break-up with Sarah because she tells him, while under truth serum, that they have no future; in Season 2, Chuck elects to break-up with Sarah again, but this time he is the one suggesting they have no future. Chuck explains, "I'd still know nothing about you," including Sarah's real name and first love, before summarizing, "I'm a normal guy…who wants a normal life…and as amazing as you are, Sarah Walker, we both know that…you will never be normal."

However, the rationales given for the respective break-ups also turn out to be equally invalid. In Season 1, Sarah simply lies about her real feelings despite the Pentothal due to her training, as she later implies to Casey. Similarly, in Season 2, Chuck, contradicts his prior claim when explicitly stating that he in fact does know Sarah and that she in fact is normal by the end of the very next episode (vs. the Cougars). After observing the insecurities lingering from Sarah's teen years, Chuck declines her remarkable offer to ask a question about her ferociously guarded past, explaining, "I don't need to know more about who you were, 'cuz as much as you don't think so, I know who you are: a girl I'd like to share a cheeseburger with." And they proceed to do exactly that. If casually sharing a cheeseburger off hours in Sarah's room doesn't qualify as a date with a normal girl, what does?

But the incongruities keep spreading. When Chuck initially decides to break-up with Sarah in Season 2, he does so under duress, partly due to the insistence of Bryce Larkin, and the issue spurring it has nothing to do with what he actually tells her at the fountain. His alleged motivation was to protect both Sarah and himself since her feelings for Chuck had evidently grown so deep that they were beginning to affect her ability to function in the field. Thus, Chuck's rationale of wanting a normal life and girl that he can know constitutes either a false pretext used to soften the blow or a delusion. If the latter, it adds yet one more layer of reversal: Sarah and Chuck trade places in flip-flopping over their feelings for one another in Season 2.

Finally, the Jill Arc (Episodes 6-8) features its own laundry list of ironic inversions, too many to cite in total. Many of the most significant examples display parallels with the past. Most obvious, Chuck must deal with his past with Jill before he can move forward with Sarah in Season 2, just as Sarah must deal with her past with Bryce before she can move forward with Chuck in Season 1. Likewise, just as Chuck helplessly watches Bryce and Sarah work as an amazing team taking out the bad guys in Season 1, Sarah looks on without a role in Season 2 as Chuck and Jill impressively decipher the music puzzle, which could be a bomb, to obtain the flash drive containing the list of Fulcrum agents. Later, Jill submits to a lie detector test, just as Sarah was exposed to truth serum, and in both cases, they lie about a future with Chuck and leave him mislead. Sarah says no, but Chuck is unaware of her ability to lie in that situation. Jill says yes, but Chuck isn't watching when the delayed result finally registers on the lie detector. Talk about déjà vu.

Among the remaining reversals evident in the Jill Arc, one deserves special attention. As noted above, a case can be made for Chuck trading places with Sarah in Season 2 when it comes to deluding himself regarding his feelings and their relationship. This seems evident during his short-lived romance with his Stanford ex and stands in marked contrast to how Sarah will deal with the aggressive beef cake Cole Barker in subsequent episodes. Jill's code name, Sand Storm, recalls Bryce Larkin's Operation Sand Wall. While Bryce posed a somewhat longer-term barrier to Sarah's feelings for Chuck that eroded over time (see Chapter 6: Sand Wall), Jill moves in and out of Chuck's emotional life more rapidly, but as she does so, the emotional storm temporarily throws dust in his eyes. Indeed, Chuck exults in finally having a "normal" girl with whom he "can have something real…together." To none other than Sarah, he explains, "And not to bash on our cover, but I've forgotten what it's like to be with someone who knows the real me" (vs. the Fat Lady).

Ironically, Jill knows Chuck all too well, and manipulates his exposed insecurities and feelings to achieve her devious goals. By the time she is through with him, Chuck's emotional world is like the hall of mirrors in which Jill and Fulcrum's Leader stalk him at the carnival: a confusion of appearances and realities that reduce Chuck to a phantom of his normal self. The lens figures this latter reality during the scene in which

Chuck's misguided feelings later lead him to steal the flash drive from Castle and flee at Sarah's muzzle point to 'save' Jill (vs. the Fat Lady). Sarah cannot bring herself to shoot Chuck, much to Casey's chagrin, and as Chuck stands facing Sarah, the glass door between them, the camera focuses on Chuck's distinct reflection next to her face (it actually looks superimposed). The camera angle doesn't even show Chuck's body; all Sarah sees in the frame is his phantom image. Likewise, the camera, when positioned behind Sarah, shows her figure in a more distant reflection beyond the back of her head, and her reflection remains even after Chuck has fled the building. This implies either that her dream of a future normal life with Chuck is growing distant or that it held her finger on the trigger. Regardless, the anguish on her face is clear.

Ultimately, the "real" Chuck rematerializes after he observes Jill taking a bead on Sarah at the Buy More. Luring Jill into lockdown in the Nerd Herd car, Chuck subsequently—and yes, ironically—inverts the prior dynamic by "breaking up" with the girl who earlier dumped him at Stanford. By the time Chuck arrives home for dinner as a "Thanksgiving Miracle," he is finally able to affirm to Ellie, "Jill, Stanford, and Bryce: that's a story from my past…But my new story is you and Sarah."

These are only a few of the ironic inversions found in the first half of Season 2, and many more are still to come. As a whole, the motif underscores "Chuck's" preoccupation with two key themes: what you see is not always what you get, and what goes around often comes around.

CHAPTER 6:

Sand Wall

From his assumed 'death' in the series pilot to his actual death in the Season 2 finale, Bryce Larkin casts a long shadow over the first two seasons of "Chuck." Throughout this tenure, he is presented as a consummate spy in every respect and a hard man with whom to compete. As for his appearance, his handsome features are accented by the cliché accents of his apparel. When not modeling non-Intersect sunglasses, he departs for missions in a tuxedo and a real bow tie, in pointed contrast to Chuck's clip-on imitation. And the Bondesque music to which he rolls doesn't hurt. But Bryce is more than just decorative wrapping.

From the viewer's first glimpse of him, Bryce exudes confidence, courage, and talent. His entry and (almost) escape from the Intersect compound in the pilot seems a superhuman display of gymnastics, and without the Intersect. When not sliding under tables or hurtling through elevated windows, Bryce plummets multiple stories on to roof tops, all the while his shirt soaked with blood. On a flashback mission with Sarah, he mingles romance with gunfire and even encourages Sarah to take a shot at the villain next to his own head without flinching (vs. the Break-Up). Bryce reprises the hero role again and again as he, teaming with Agent Walker, takes out Fulcrum agents with choreographed perfection in the Buy More (vs. the Nemesis) and battles Roark's men at Ellie's first wedding (vs. the Ring). Meanwhile, Chuck cowers behind the nearest piece of furniture. Moreover, at Ellie's wedding Bryce doesn't even flinch before offering himself to Roark in exchange for everyone else.

It isn't all roses, though. Like Sarah and even Casey, Bryce suffers the loneliness and disorientation of the espionage world. At the Buy More (vs. the Nemesis), before Bryce is about to "disappear" once again after his transfer to CIA custody, Chuck calls him "the super spy," but Bryce's reply is revealing: "It's nothing. I've got one friend in this world....You've got a home and a store full of them." And while they stand in front of a bank of flat screens, notably projecting images from an ocean underworld, Bryce further comments, "These HD screens almost look like the real thing," suggesting his prolonged detachment from the normal world has altered his ability to distinguish it from his spy reality. This detachment is echoed at Ellie's wedding on the beach. While friends and family gather to participate, Bryce observes remotely behind a sand dune at such a distance he requires binoculars to see and an earpiece to communicate. And that's when there is someone to communicate with. In Operation Sand Wall, his cover proves so deep that even Sarah, his partner and lover, thinks that he has gone rogue, and he must contrive a means of taking Chuck hostage in a full-security interrogation facility just to integrate himself back into the CIA...and hopefully Sarah's heart.

Chuck's relationship with Bryce is ironic as well. The name for Bryce's prior mission, Operation Sand Wall, is precisely named, for though Bryce does present barriers to Chuck, they ultimately wash away. Most obvious, Bryce's actions at Stanford cause a relational separation of a few years, but in the end the truth largely erodes it. For much of Season 1, Chuck regards Bryce as his primary enemy, the guy that got him kicked out of college for cheating and stole his girlfriend for good measure, leaving Chuck in a pit of self-pity. Bryce's faux betrayals trigger a general life tailspin that finds Chuck without a degree, making $11 an hour fixing computers with the riff raff, and talking to potential dates about how Bryce ruined his life at his party in the pilot. As Chuck himself articulates when asked at his party in the pilot, "I'm working on my five-year plan, just need to choose a font." Upon learning that Chuck still lives with his sister, even Bryce asks, "Chuck, what happened to you? Guy that wanted to be the sophomore billionaire, Bill Gates with style" (vs. the Nemesis). At the time, all Chuck can muster in reply is to remind Bryce he got him kicked out of Stanford.

Chuck's lack of motivation and direction for the future do eventually evaporate, though, as he discovers his talents and virtues, sometimes even playing the role of hero in the hidden spy world. Chuck receives his tardy Stanford degree, thanks to Sarah, and even finds himself in the ironic position of dumping Jill after the misguided resumption of their relationship (see Chapter 5: Symmetries and Ironies). And when Chuck discovers that Bryce acted to protect him from the CIA at Stanford, Chuck feels compelled to walk back out to the dumpster and retrieve the fraternity photo in which he stands smiling with his arm around Bryce's shoulders (vs. the Alma Mater). In his last words to his mortally wounded frat brother in the Intersect white room, Chuck actually pleads with Bryce to hold on so Bryce and Sarah can go out and save the world.

Still, when Bryce suddenly reappears in Episodes 9-10 of Season 1, Chuck's friend also returns as a rival for Sarah's affection. Ironically, it is in front of Bryce's life support cell that the Nerd Herder and Sarah stand when their romance finally manifests itself in the form of that first kiss she plants on Chuck (vs. the Imported Hard Salami), but Bryce's subsequent resurrection from that cell threatens to put Chuck's blooming relationship with her in the grave. And when Chuck shows up per the advice of Roan Montgomery with a bottle of wine, a single rose, and a white dinner jacket, Bryce greets him at Sarah's door asking, "Miss me?" (vs. the Seduction). This competitive dynamic is figured when Bryce and Chuck stand side by side in the Buy More, seeking Sarah's attention, after Bryce shoots Chuck wearing the vest and speaking a little Klingon (vs. the Nemesis). Both also follow Sarah with their eyes as she, too conflicted to speak, silently skirts past them. Season 2 offers a similar image (vs. the Break-Up): the two suitors groom themselves in front of the mirror in the hotel room, subtly probing the other's motives until facing Sarah when she appears.

Chuck's angst over Sarah's feelings for Bryce isn't without foundation, for his emerging relationship with Sarah follows a steamy one with Bryce that was suddenly put on hold. When not flashing back to missions mixing kisses with muzzle flashes, Sarah, thinking Bryce dead in the pilot, wistfully scrolls through cell phone pictures of her vacation with him in Cabo. Notably, when Bryce surprises Sarah in Chuck's room, he claims Sarah won't arrest him because she's still in love with him, and she in fact can't resist his pass at her, admitting, "You've still got it." Exquisite teamwork as spies complements and perhaps fuels their passion. The flashback mission matches their symmetrical, slo-mo destruction of the Fulcrum agents in the Buy More (vs. the Nemesis), displaying a bad-assedness so impressive that even Chuck has to admit, "Wow! They really are great." And Bryce is quick to remind Sarah of their former lives as the slick spy couple Mr. and Mrs. Anderson, even slipping a ring back on her finger after strutting into Castle prior to a mission.

However, the question increasingly becomes: where does Bryce fit into Sarah's present? Clues suggest that Sarah's relationship with Bryce is of a different variety than the one she builds with Chuck. Compared to the guy who "is making it his mission to know me" (vs. Sarah), Bryce comes off as a bit ignorant of Sarah's tastes. While Bryce sends a florist's shop to the hospitalized Sarah in "vs. the Break-Up," Chuck, the one who knows that Sarah doesn't like olives but does like extra pickles, brings a humble bouquet of gardenias. A smiling Sarah wonders, "They are my favorite. How did you know?" Then again, as Bryce affirms, Sarah was "never good at…the saying your feelings part" (vs. the Nemesis), which presents a challenge even to Chuck. But the often rambling Nerd Herder still extracts more from Sarah's carefully guarded thoughts. Interestingly, even at the start of "vs. the Break-Up" Bryce remains unaware of the genuine romantic dynamic between Chuck and Sarah, something she has clearly kept him in the dark about. In perhaps the most notable difference, Bryce, as his last name suggests, represents a lark to Sarah, an ongoing action-adventure part- nership that takes her to exotic and varied destinations. However, as Sarah's priorities change and Chuck provides a link to her closely guarded dream of a future normal life, it places a potentially itinerant life with Bryce, no matter how exciting, within a different frame (see Chapter 4: A Slow and Painful Awakening).

Indeed, like the professional aspects of Chuck's life, Bryce proves only a temporary barrier to his romance with Sarah. In retrospect, the end of Bryce's passionate lark with Sarah was signaled. About to leave the Buy More in his tux for his deep cover Intersect mission in "vs. the Nemesis," Bryce tells Chuck, "…Bryce Larkin is dead…and it's going to stay that way this time." Similarly, when pointedly on the verge of making another pass at Sarah in the back seat of the CIA transport, the moment is rudely inter- rupted by the crash with the Fulcrum vehicle, and the couple lays 'dead' on the pavement until they see an opening. The episode ends with Sarah looking up from Chuck's face on her cell phone and staring ahead to the future, not looking back to the phone call from Bryce ringing beside her.

And Sarah never does look back. When Bryce stops in to the Orange Orange to resurrect their relationship in Season 2 (vs. the Break-Up), Sarah notably busies herself with wiping down the glass fixtures even as she has already wiped away their romantic past. As Bryce flirtatiously addresses Mrs. Anderson, Sarah politely but firmly urges him to "keep it strictly a cover this time." When Bryce persists, taking her hand and musing, "…It was fun while it lasted," Sarah does not reply verbally, and her non-verbal reaction doesn't encourage him. It gets no more promising from there.

Sarah proceeds to show more concern over Chuck's disappointment in how she looks for the mission, criticizes Bryce's "rusty" dance skills, and, symbolically, refuses to let him lead the tango. Thoroughly professional, though, they still manage to sell their lascivious masquerade to the point a waiter suggests they "get a room."

Bryce's ultimate awakening to Sarah's affection for Chuck, confirmed by Dr. Awesome as he treats Bryce's cuts at the hospital, is painful (vs. the Break-Up). Each revelation Awesome provides, even as he cleans the dirt from Bryce's face, is accompanied by a pronounced "Ouch!" Awesome adds the exclamation point: "Cut's pretty deep." Even at the end of the season, when Bryce appears one last time, slated to work with Sarah on the new phase of the Intersect project upon Chuck's announced exit from the CIA, Sarah betrays not an inkling of interest in rekindling their passion. When he appears in Castle, Sarah never moves to engage him, instead remaining fixed, her forward-focused, strained face betraying thoughts of Chuck and foreshadowing her ultimate decision not to leave with Bryce, even as a mere professional partner (vs. the Ring). Though he initially asserts Sarah "can finally get out of [Burbank]," Bryce ultimately admits he has lost Sarah to Chuck. Not only does he inform Chuck that Sarah is not leaving with him on the Intersect mission, but Bryce tells the Fulcrum double agent Sarah "loves another guy" just minutes before his death in the Intersect white room, adding with dramatic irony, "Bad day to be me."

Within this context, Bryce's coded invitation for Sarah to join him on the Intersect mission, like the mission code name Sand Wall, also foreshadows the outcome. On the verge of going off-grid, he signals, "Sarah, we'll always have Omaha," even as the same music ("No One's Gonna Love You" by Band of Horses) is cued and will continue to play through the scene in which Sarah declines to answer his phone call. Though "Omaha" references Bryce's Intersect-related mission from his Stanford days, which may or may not have involved Sarah, the phrase also implies a second meaning. As a World War II D-Day invasion allusion, it further figures that Bryce may have succeeded in gaining a tentative beachhead on Sarah's heart but was unable to penetrate further and occupy it, as Chuck does. Appropriately, Sarah's last sight of Bryce still alive, pointedly on another beach at Ellie's wedding, presents him standing in the distance with binoculars, scouting the terrain of a real life as a spectator from behind a sand wall.

CHAPTER 7:

Thunder and Rain

It is no exaggeration to say that "Chuck vs. the Santa Claus," placed mid-way through Season 2, serves as a crucial episode in terms of tracking the development of the relationship between Chuck and Sarah. Given its deep texturing, often echoing other episodes and motifs in the series, the text requires a particularly close reading of five scenes to fully illuminate it.

The first scene, which includes Sarah's preparation for opening at the Orange Orange and Chuck dropping in with an invitation to a Bartowski Christmas, presents a critical framework through which to view the balance of the episode. The scene begins with the foregrounding of the seemingly mundane: pointedly working behind the transparent glass fixture, implying a window into her thoughts, Sarah places two pairs of tongs in the toppings display before unstacking a set of cups and rearranging them in a row on top of the glass fixture. Far from incidental, the highlighting of this task foreshadows an imminent internal rearrangement necessary for Sarah to hold on to her dream of a normal future (see Chapter 2: Fish Out of Water).

On cue, the advertisement on the far wall captures her attention and causes her to pause. Featuring a photo of a family enjoying eggnog frozen yogurt, it headlines "Take Home Some Family Holiday Spirit." For emphasis, the frame pans in on the picture for a few moments before shifting back to a pensive Sarah, her expression betraying a touch of longing. This scenario mirrors a similar reverie in "vs. the Wookiee," when Sarah stares into the goldfish bowl, another moment of transparency, except this time her focus is not on her lonely past but a family-oriented future. Moreover, just as Sarah returns to her hotel room from a 'family' game night at the Bartowski's in "vs. the Wookiee," Chuck arrives precisely on time to interrupt her private thoughts with an invitation to a family Christmas at the Bartowski's. As Chuck strolls in, Sarah's face remains somewhat fixed, but her eyes follow him as he approaches the counter, further linking her personal Intersection with the real world to her thoughts prompted by the ad on the wall.

After delivering his invitation, Chuck seems taken aback by Sarah's announcement that she doesn't "do" Christmas. But the ad is still on her mind. Clearly conflicted, Sarah claims she doesn't "want to get into it," but her body language does not match her words: she promptly turns to face him, slides up on the counter across from him, and has every appearance of settling in to do just that. In fact, moments later Sarah is freely divulging another chunk of her unlovely past to Chuck, specifically the annual Salvation Army con job on Christmas Eve. One need only reflect back to "vs. the Cougars" to realize the growth in transparency this demonstrates in Sarah—as well as her unique trust in Chuck, who assured her he didn't need to know anything more about her past to know who she is now: a normal girl. Significantly, Chuck reaffirms this view in this scene: "I'm not buying the whole Scrooge act, OK? Underneath that spy cover is a regular person just like the rest of us." Before he leaves, Chuck rattles off the Christmas traditions observed in the Bartowski family, refuses to accept no for an answer, and warns her, "Prepare to be heart-warmed." Disarmed, and privately gratified, Sarah is left able only to smile and playfully throw a piece of paper at her charmer.

The second scene shifts the drama into high gear. After the Buy More is taken hostage, Casey and Sarah attempt to extract Chuck, but he refuses, citing his unwillingness to abandon family and friends and ends up dragging his handlers into captivity as well. Ned, the hostage taker, eventually allows the gesture of calling a loved one, and after a series of comic cameos showing others accepting the offer, the camera focuses on the erstwhile goldfish, Sarah, pointedly with no one to call, wistfully observing others while slowly shuffling through the aisles. But Chuck does call, from the privacy of the romantic comedy DVD's, no less.

Chuck crouches, and Sarah kneels, creating an intimate, vulnerable mood. Not coincidentally, Sarah softly directs the conversation to family....and them: "So, Ned let everyone call their loved ones. That was pretty smart to call me...protect our cover." Sarah's disappointment with the irony is tangible in tone and expression, and Chuck picks up on the theme, highlighting the ambiguity: "Yeah, well, you are my girlfriend...

sort of." Lightly flirtatious, Sarah asks if the Christmas invitation still stands, revealing her openness to heart-warming, and the easy, mutual affection is palpable. That is until Chuck makes his own revelation and dispels the ambiguity.

While announcing he has a present for Sarah, Chuck's expression grows uncharacteristically serious, even burdened. Still in the midst of grasping his words and demeanor, Sarah observes Chuck pull out a small jewelry bag, and her own expression shifts from quiet longing to slightly startled, her mouth unhinging. Initially reassuring Chuck, "We're gonna get out of here. We'll be fine…," her voice suddenly trails off with emotion as she sees Chuck draw the charm bracelet out from the bag and hold it before her eyes. She is barely able to voice the end of her sentence: "I promise." The pointed linking of these words with the bracelet calls attention to the deeper significance of the gift. Stunned, taken by surprise, even a tad embarrassed, Sarah can only shrug her shoulders. But a smile begins to fill her face before she continues, "Wow! That's beautiful."

Still, when Chuck notably reveals the family history of the bracelet, Sarah balks, but as in the Orange Orange, her words fail to match her actions. "Oh, Chuck, I can't take this," she protests, but as he delicately wraps and latches it around her outstretched, upturned wrist, Sarah makes no effort to withdraw her hand. "This is something real," she adds, "something that you should give to a real girlfriend," but all the while she allows Chuck to continue caressing her hand. A sheepish look on his face, Chuck pauses before replying, signaling that when he does, he does so with a full comprehension of all it conveys: "I know." Sarah's eyes lock on Chuck's before she lowers her head, trying to grasp Chuck's dramatic gesture: cover or not, Sarah is his real girlfriend, and the bracelet is his promise of pursuing a real future life with her. Chuck has clearly come a long way from his monologue at the fountain in "vs. the Break-Up." And if sharing a cheeseburger with Sarah at the close of "vs. the Cougars" signaled the unofficial end to their 'break-up,' this moment several episodes later serves as the official notification. After Chuck leaves to deal further with Ned, the lens remains on the private Sarah still staring ahead in disbelief, but no sign of regret, then down to look at the bracelet chain once more, trying to absorb the tangible evidence that her dream of a future family and normal life may now actually have links to reality.

Sarah was not prepared to accept such a gesture at the end of Season 1. In fact, she rejected one substantially like it in "vs. the Marlin" when Chuck and Sarah lurked outside the window spying on Awesome's marriage proposal (see Chapter 4: A Slow and Painful Awakening). Sarah declined joining Chuck's invitation to join him inside, citing it a "family time." When Chuck replied with the exact same words, "I know," Sarah politely changed the subject and bid him good night. The imagery of Sarah extending her upturned wrist to Chuck also bears note. In one regard, it resonates with a scene from "vs. the Cougars" as well as the tree lot scene with Mauser later in "vs. the Santa Claus." When Graham offers the young Jenny Burton salvation in the form of working for the CIA in a flashback, she initially confuses it with imprisonment and surrenders herself to Graham in a similar manner: outstretched hands and upturned wrists. Mauser repeats the image with Sarah in a pronounced manner. Within this context, Sarah's posture in accepting the bracelet likely indicates a willful surrender to her dream of a normal future in general, and one with Chuck in particular. The balance of the episode bears this out.

When circumstances require the release of Casey and Sarah, Sarah's parting with Chuck emphasizes the immediate effect of Chuck's gesture on her. When she hugs him with feeling, the camera angle prominently displaying the bracelet dangling from her wrist, she holds him silently for a moment before speaking into his ear, her expression earnest. After receiving Chuck's gift and the promise it implies, she has a private pledge of her own to whisper in return: "Trust me; I'll never let anyone hurt you." And she won't, even long after Mauser is six feet under. Before Season 2 ends, Sarah will again whisper in Chuck's ear on almost the very spot they currently occupy (vs. the First Kill), and in doing so she will save him from Beckman's bunker even if it means committing treason.

The preceding scenes provide the context necessary to interpret the climactic events in the Christmas tree lot. The late December night air in Burbank is crisp, another instance of the hot and cold motif that implies imminent danger to Chuck and Sarah, too, since he is the source of Sarah's heart-warming. Before the rain starts falling, the thunder in the distance foreshadows the approach of a tumultuous event. Sarah, locating

Chuck before Mauser, silences Chuck with her hand over his mouth, the positioning of the camera once again drawing attention to the bracelet on her wrist, this time the heart pendant prominent. At Sarah's insistence, Chuck begins to head back to the Buy More and safety, only to rethink matters and become a secret spectator.

The ensuing fight between Sarah and Mauser ends with Sarah holding the gun, but that doesn't stop his mockery. Fulcrum has won, he insists. The identity of Chuck Bartowski has been revealed, and there is no cell solitary enough to keep the word from getting out. And when it does, it will mean "the end of [Chuck's] pathetic existence." A baptismal rain begins to fall as Sarah grapples with the sudden complexities of the situation and the life-altering consequences stemming from her impending decision. Mauser reaches out his hands in surrender, prior to holding them outstretched to the sides in a sacrificial pose, and then back in front. The ethics of shooting an unarmed man are problematic for a CIA handler, though not necessarily indefensible. But sparing Mauser's life will likely, in the end, sacrifice the life of Chuck and those he cares for...as well as her own dream, if she is finally ready to step into the shower (see Chapter 2).

Questions surely fill Sarah's mind. What future does she want? One filled with an incessant string of solitary nights in the country and hotel du jour, or one promising Christmases at the Bartowski's? This time, unlike her passive choice between two phone calls, safeguarding the possibility of a real future will require her to act. Her face strains. She swallows hard. Her lips purse. In or out? Just before she pulls the trigger, Sarah's face betrays the same defiant expression as young Jenny Burton when cornered by Graham, her lips bulging. The camera confirms the tale: slowly panning down from the smoking barrel, the frame finally and pointedly rests on the ever-present bracelet dangling from her wrist, the heart pendant again prominent. The finger that pulled the trigger was not merely that of a handler but also that of a real girlfriend and a dreamer.

The aftermath gives further insight into the significance of Chuck's and Sarah's exchange of promises. Sarah enters the Buy More, her eyes searching for Chuck, face tentative, almost blank. When she spots him, her expression is best described as exhausted relief: he's there, safe. Her eyes linger on him a few moments longer before her expression shifts to something akin to joy as she springs back into action. "Chuck!" Sarah bounds up to him and finds his lips, both hands to his face, followed by a hug and, seemingly, a sigh. When she steps back, she smiles, her face animated. Speaking as much to herself as to Chuck, Sarah assures her real cover boyfriend, "It's OK. You're safe. I got the Fulcrum agent." Enamored with the moment and reconciled to her decision in the tree lot, she fails to detect the angst in Chuck's expression as he reacts to her lie and continues, "It's OK! He's going to go to jail. He's never going to bother you again."

Sarah's outward reaction to the gift and all it represents only seems to grow more unguarded before the credits roll. Sarah proceeds to model the bracelet for her potential future sister-in-law, smiling, her full eyes returning to meet Chuck's, then down to the bracelet again. Her demeanor implies that her surrender to the dream, and Chuck, is already captivating her as she considers the prospects of a rearranged life.

Of course, Chuck and Sarah's relationship will not enjoy a straight trajectory to "vs. the Honeymooners" (mid-way through Season 3) and beyond. Indeed, many struggles and temporary detours loom ahead. The first, Chuck's disillusionment over Sarah's execution of Mauser and lying about it, is introduced before episode's end. Chuck will also naively chase alternative dreams, and Sarah's prowling fears will resurrect. As Chuck says while dividing that cheeseburger with Sarah in "vs. the Cougars," "This is going to be messy." But "vs. the Santa Claus" remains a definitive, unambiguous text that promises Chuck and Sarah will ultimately both strive for a real life together.

CHAPTER 8:

A Tale of Two Handlers

Dictionaries define a "handler" in a variety of ways, ranging from "one who manages or trains a subject" to "one who manipulates." As Chuck's CIA handler, Sarah covers both definitions while developing Chuck into a productive intelligence asset—and spy. However, Sarah's professional occupation also serves as a loose controlling metaphor figuring the private management of Chuck as her personal asset for much of the series and especially in Season 2. Increasingly, Sarah proves compelled to 'handle' Chuck-related matters that extend far beyond her official duties, revealing motives far from exploitive while doing so.

From early in the pilot, the new Intersect struggles with self-confidence, a fact that causes him to stumble in his forward progress in life. Still crippled by the events that unfolded at Stanford, both academic and romantic, he claims he's working on a 5-year plan and undecided on the font (Pilot). Sensing Chuck's untapped potential, Sarah unofficially adopts a secondary mission to coach Chuck into re-framing his view of himself and realizing his capabilities (see Chapter 1: Water Lillies).

Over time, Sarah becomes sensitized to the extent to which Chuck's classified dismissal from Stanford has psychologically and professionally crippled him. Consequently, Sarah secretly negotiates with authorities to award Chuck his Stanford diploma (vs. Tom Sawyer). Despite Chuck's initial skepticism upon receiving it, Sarah helps Chuck to see how much his varied and noteworthy service to the CIA has more than made up for his missing credits, especially given his CIA-induced expulsion, and firmly states, "You earned it, Chuck." Additionally, knowing how much Chuck's secret life gnaws at him since family and friends can view him solely from outside the spy-life framework, she ensures that Ellie is aware of the achievement and concocts the story that Chuck finished his degree online to surprise her.

Similarly, Sarah encourages Chuck when it is time to use that degree to temporarily obtain his dream job (vs. the Dream Job) at Roark Industries. When Chuck's insecurities about his impending interview begin to surface, Sarah assures her personal asset, "You're going in as Charles Bartowski: your name, your resume, your Stanford degree," adding, "You're perfectly qualified to go in as yourself." And while Chuck begins to hedge during the interview, Sarah, linked by earpiece, again affirms her faith in him, urging, "Chuck, just be honest." Bolstered by her support, Chuck finds the courage to speak the truth: "...I would say probably my greatest weakness is how little I've pushed myself since college. I've been trapped in a job, a life that I don't really want but don't really see a way out." Even as Sarah reacts with emotion in the van, she is proven right: Chuck is offered the job on his own merits. In the aftermath, Chuck regrets that he didn't take such risks sooner, alleging that if he had done so, his dad, supposedly unaware of his double life, wouldn't consider him "a loser." Again, Sarah disputes his claim, arguing, "Chuck, he knows you're not a loser." And when Chuck persists, clarifying, "Well, something more than Nerd Herding," Sarah insists, "You *are*."

Sarah concerns herself with Chuck's private profile as well. In "vs. Tom Sawyer," Ellie voices concern over Chuck's apparent aimlessness, noting, "It's like he's slipping back into old Chuck mode. You know, no confidence, no direction....And he went to Stanford, for God's sake. Did you know he was 12 credits short of...a real life[?]" Sarah responds by building him up without revealing his cover: "You know, Chuck is, a, Chuck is like a duck. Sometimes it seems like he is just gliding along, but beneath the surface his little feet are just paddling away like crazy. Deep down, I really think Chuck is an incredibly mature and responsible guy." Of course, Chuck walks in at that moment with a passed-out Jeff over his shoulder! Likewise, when Sarah's father labels Chuck "a shnook" before Chuck arrives to meet Sarah and him for dinner, Sarah passionately counters, "He's not a shnook! He's a wonderful, caring, intelligent guy."

Truth be known, from early in Season 1 forward Sarah views Chuck as more than just capable, but as a hero and consistently tries to get Chuck to recognize his exceptional quality, too. Just before Sarah admits she could endure a forced kiss in "vs. the Tango," Chuck laments, "What's the good of being a hero if no one knows about it?" Already a cheerleader in the third episode, Sarah replies, "Well, you know it…and I know it, too." Additionally, Sarah smiles from ear to ear at the end of "vs. Tom Sawyer" after Chuck proves the first to reach the kill screen and obtain the satellite code that averts a possible nuclear confrontation. As the crowd at the Buy More celebrates the world's new Missile Command champion, a widely smiling Sarah asks, "What does it feel like to be a hero, Mr. Bartowski?" Chuck even impresses none other than veteran and formerly skeptical spy Roan Montgomery (vs. the Seduction). After Chuck's swashbuckling leap from the Buy More rooftop to save Sarah from the Black Widow, Montgomery openly gushes, "Now that's a spy!" This anticipates Sarah lavishing perhaps the ultimate compliment: "I have to admit, that was pretty impressive….I think it's safe to say, Chuck, that I've never seen anyone quite like you."

Pointedly, Sarah handles not only Chuck's psyche but, in Season 2, also their relationship, specifically in terms of keeping open the possibility of a real future with him. Indeed, Sarah further links the hero's journey on which she is coaching Chuck to their future together because she sees it, potentially, as the only means of ultimately achieving a permanent relationship with him when he is no longer an intelligence asset without her leaving the CIA. This well-meaning if ulterior motive begins to reveal itself in "vs. the First Date." While following Chuck out to the courtyard after he learns that the new Intersect is almost online—and his return to normal life seemingly near--Sarah appears particularly concerned with expanding his horizons. When Chuck says, "I don't think I'm really cut out for a job where you disarm a bomb, steal a diamond, and jump off a building," Sarah replies, "Well, you could have fooled me." After Chuck proceeds to discount her comments and mentions the Buy More as part of his future, Sarah can't help but interrupt: "Chuck, can I tell you something?...You can do anything. I've seen you in action, and I'm not just talking about the bomb diffusing or the diamond stealing. I mean, anything you wanted you could have." Sarah's leading tone and expression accent her meaning. Even before the episode concludes, she accepts two dates.

In the next episode, Sarah echoes similar, thinly-veiled sentiments to entice the aggrieved Chuck to take the Roan Montgomery mission: "The sooner we get the cypher back, the sooner you can have the Intersect removed and the sooner you can be free to live whatever life you choose with whomever you choose." When Chuck insists on clarification, Sarah makes a strikingly overt statement with doe eyes: "I'm saying you could have everything that you always wanted." Three episodes later (vs. Tom Sawyer), Sarah sings the same tune. Pointing out the burning satellite in the starry evening sky, she urges Chuck to "Make a wish; it's yours." Since both look at the other longingly when the other isn't looking, it's not difficult to read their minds. Clearly, these are not manipulations of a merely ambitious handler.

With the progression of Season 2, Sarah further handles the relationship by trying to safeguard that potential future. As much as the Jill Arc proves an interruption to Chuck and Sarah's relationship, Sarah's behavior remains entirely noble throughout. Keeping her own angst hidden from Chuck, she speaks well of Jill publicly, well of Chuck to Jill privately, and tells Casey that Chuck both "deserves a real girlfriend" and his privacy to pursue the relationship. When Jill takes herself out of the picture, Sarah's selfless loyalty smooths the path to Chuck's gift of the bracelet in "vs. the Santa Claus." Moreover, after her status of real girlfriend is established (see Chapter 7: Thunder and Rain), she makes every effort to protect the relationship when Chuck occasionally threatens to wander off that path.

Indeed, unlike her pained, passive acceptance at the fountain in "vs. the Breakup," Sarah actively attempts to avert a breakup she sees looming and even takes proactive steps on multiple occasions. In no segment of the series does this initiative-taking evidence itself more than the two episodes presenting the English hunk of a spy, Cole Barker (vs. the Beefcake & vs. the Lethal Weapon). Tipped off by the surveillance of Chuck's apartment, Sarah repeatedly calls Chuck and even catches him screening her calls at the Buy More. Persistent, she invites Chuck over to the shop for frozen yogurt and matter-of-factly brings the matter to a point when Chuck seems reticent to do so: "You want to break up again?" While Chuck proceeds to lament how "complicated" his double life has become, Sarah's expression dampens before she notably takes off a glove and recites a rehearsed speech. "Look," she begins with regained composure, "Tell them we're taking things slowly and that, while we enjoy each other's company, we don't really see the need to label it." However, the words begin to spill out more quickly near the end; and her nervous head tilt, glassy eyes, set jaw, and nearly-cracking voice evidence a struggle to keep her composure. After Chuck softly presses home the undisputed opinion that they will "never really be together,"

Sarah's inability to conceal her disappointment in front of him proves unprecedented. With searching eyes, her expression a tad too brave, Sarah cannot hide the appeal in her voice: "Is that what you really want?" When Chuck answers with certainty, Sarah pointedly turns back to the glass case, her mouth transparently open with grief.

Sarah's heart continues to fight for her future with Chuck near the end of the same episode (vs. the Beefcake), despite Barker's amazing heroism, self-assurance, good looks, and flirtatious manner. First offering congratulations to Chuck on his enduring torture, Sarah once more manipulates the light-hearted banter about Chuck's "ticklish toes" towards a serious conversation about them: "…You've had a lot of practice enduring torture…with our fake relationship." Chuck pauses, reflecting on her words for a few moments before replying, "You know, it wasn't completely torture….We certainly had our moments, didn't we?" Before Sarah responds, a more wistful expression replaces her smile. Briefly lowering her gaze, Sarah's eyes return to meet Chuck's, her lips set as they huskily voice a coded confession: "Well, even though it wasn't real…I'm really going to miss it." Deciphering Sarah's irony, Chuck struggles before speaking. But in the midst of revealing that he may have "made an impulsive decision," Barker interrupts and the moment is fractured. Sarah's video log entry (Day 564), featuring her Orange Orange outfit, is likely recorded around this time or soon thereafter, and this period fits: Sarah is certainly acting like someone who is finally admitting to herself, "I'm in love with Chuck Bartowski, and I don't know what to do about it."

In "vs. the Lethal Weapon," Sarah's handling focus shifts to guarding their very real cover relationship. In a private moment, Sarah, who attempts to keep an emotional wall between her and Barker throughout the episode, cannot resist when he leaps over that wall in the form of a forceful pass at her. Though severely tested, Sarah regroups a day or two later, toothbrush in hand, to firmly assure an inquisitive (and voyeuristic) Chuck, "Ah, our connection was purely professional. That's it," her eyes looking directly into his. Undeterred by Sarah's subsequent cool behavior, Barker comes on strong one last time. And after hearing the Bondesque beefcake pine for her and even invite her on a spontaneous, passionate lark, Sarah takes the precaution of walking away, consciously creating distance to avert another pass, before answering, "I guess I'm not the kind of girl who cheats on her cover boyfriend." In response, Barker muses incredulously, "Cole Barker loses the girl to Chuck Bartowski," and Sarah does not deny it. Instead, she respectfully throws Barker's words back at him: "When you meet somebody you care about, it's just hard to walk away."

Sarah's inability to walk away from her precious private asset receives the ultimate test in "vs. the First Kill," and the stake is not another man but her career. Though she initially and uncharacteristically challenges Beckman's order to bunker Chuck in the wake of his father's capture by Fulcrum, Sarah dutifully enters the Buy More to do Beckman's bidding, mask firmly in place, and lie to Chuck to ensure his cooperation. However, Sarah is once again confronted with a clarification by crisis. With her whole life as she knows it riding on the line, she comes to realize that burning the intelligence asset will also result in burning her personal asset, who admits his eroding trust in her. That option is simply not acceptable, regardless of the professional consequences. Perhaps recalling her whispered promise to never let anyone hurt him, made on almost precisely the same spot in "vs. the Santa Claus," Sarah chooses Chuck and her conscience by, again, whispering in his ear.

As the chapter title implies, Sarah is not the only handler in this relationship during Season 2. When not side-tracked by Jill, the erstwhile intelligence asset is also happy to trade places and serve, famously announced in the pilot, as Sarah's "personal baggage handler," often using humor to lighten the load. Episode 4 (vs. the Cougars) highlights this dynamic, though Chuck gets off to a rocky start. Initially thinking Sarah's insecurities regarding high school merely typical, he insincerely noses his way into Sarah's past and succeeds in pushing enough of her emotional panic buttons to earn Sarah's stern warning-- "Back off!"—and watch her fire a pencil through his head in their photo across the room, shattering the glass.

However, as the episode progresses, and Chuck becomes more sensitized to the depth of her internal struggle, Sarah begins to lower her emotional walls over a well-pummeled punching bag. And after an awkward moment while picking up her name badge on her reunion mission, Chuck steps in to reassure her appealing eyes: "Hey, hey, hey, hey. No one's going to mess with you, Sarah, OK? I got your back." Then, in pure Chuck fashion, he cracks a joke that makes her laugh, and the moment passes. Chuck's continued support and the trust it engenders "earns" a replacement picture and frame to grace Sarah's side table and her offer to answer a question about her past. But in another feat of baggage handling, Chuck declines, claiming he already knows who she is now, and that's all he really cares about. At this blanket acceptance of her unlovely past and validation of her present, Sarah's face lights up with an endearing look that reveals her utter heart-warming.

Later in the season, "vs. the DeLorean" foregrounds Chuck's continued work as emotional porter when Sarah's father blows into town. After another awkward start (caught while spying on her 'date' with her dad), Chuck comes alongside Sarah and helps shoulder her burden. Torn up over the lack in her relationship with a delinquent father, who leaves town with $10 million after suckering her into trusting him, Sarah unfolds herself to Chuck once more the next morning. Sensing her mood, Chuck drops in with breakfast to check if she is "OK." Grateful for the chocolate croissants and his concern, Sarah proceeds to offer him more of her baggage in return.

"If there's one thing I learned from my father," Sarah explains, "it's be ready for disappointment," adding, "And if it's anyone's fault, it's mine." Her brief look at Chuck as she speaks the last words before looking back down tell as much about her need for Chuck's emotional management as when her eyes lock on his face while he corrects her: "No, it's not." After revealing a similar bit of his own hurtful past with his dad, Chuck concludes, "…You need to know that your father's sins are his, not yours." With notable repositioning of her head, shifting eyes, and pursing lips, Sarah lets him know his words found their mark: "That's pretty eloquent for 9:00 AM." But after sharing the heavy moment, Chuck's humor again rides in to manipulate the mood with perfect timing: "What can I say? I am an articulate shnook." Sarah's relief is palpable when she breaks into a smile and even laughs, "Lucky for me." This developing trust is symbolically replicated when the ever-self-reliant Sarah, at episode's end, willingly accepts the warmth of Chuck's jacket when chilled by the breeze…and her father's all-too-expected disappearance.

In a less light-hearted manner, Chuck the Handler also guides Sarah's integration into the normal world by providing insight into friendship (vs. the Best Friend), given her itinerate childhood lacking in long-term relationships with even parents, let alone peers. When Chuck perceives Sarah as unsympathetic to the agony he experiences when forced to not only accept a mission involving a party hosted by Morgan's rival for Anna but then embarrass Morgan in front of Anna in order to possibly save his life, he feels compelled to give Sarah a heartfelt training session while alone with her in Castle. After reviewing his life-long history with Morgan, including the darkest moments in which Morgan was there for him, Chuck asserts, "Morgan is more than just my 'best friend.'...He's my family. Before you got here...and long after you've gone, Morgan is my family." At the moment, Sarah dispassionately disputes Chuck's lesson, with some validity. By the episode's closing scene at the Buy More, though, she demonstrates she was listening: "I wanted to apologize. I could have been more sensitive before about your relationship with Morgan....It's just, it's difficult...I don't really have anyone in my life that, who...who cares about me." Of course, Chuck begs to differ and tells her so, taking her hand to accent the point.

In a final facet of the handling motif, Chuck and Sarah demonstrate decided differences in how they manage the invisible prison of the handler/asset relationship that keeps them apart and offers no guarantee of a future together. On the one hand, Sarah seems far more comfortable in their fake relationship, for it allows her to love Chuck without leaving the comfort of the only world she has known, the spy world. She is reasonably content to act out her feelings for Chuck within the confines of the cover and not have to make the looming tough choice between the spy world and the normal one. However, the tantalizing dynamic grates on Chuck, especially given his familiarity with the freedom the real world offers him.

The kisses Chuck and Sarah share serve as Exhibit A. Chuck balks at their first public kiss at the Buy More (vs. the Tango), while Sarah playfully enjoys issuing the directive and expresses disappointment when Chuck doesn't play along. In Season 2, frustrated with his reinstatement as the Intersect, especially after his first real date with Sarah, Chuck gives a relatively reserved response to the cartwheeling lioness who prowls up his tie before yanking him to another national emergency (vs. the Seduction). Even with Roan Montgomery, Chuck practices evasion tactics when instructed to kiss Sarah, while Sarah assures him "It's OK" to go for it. And the passion he experiences in the midst of that kiss only makes the cover nature of their relationship harder for Chuck to bear.

Likewise, Sarah seems to thrive in "vs. the Suburbs" when they pose as a married couple. Pleased not only to arise early to make Chuck's breakfast, she follows him to the driveway before he starts his commute so she can hand him the grocery list and wave good-bye with the dog.

Yet, after the mission is over, Sarah's behavior towards Chuck turns cool when asking for the ring back in reply to his suggestion of returning to the 'burbs for one more night. However, her reaction to taking off her own ring after supervising the clean-up of the house suggests her behavior is driven by the harshness of the return to reality.

The dynamic repeats itself in episodes where Chuck and Sarah share a bed. In Season 1, Sarah teases Chuck with lingerie and even seems to mock his frustrated response to it (vs. the Truth). A quarrel ensues, and Chuck ultimately opts for the floor. And when Barker is captured in "vs. the Lethal Weapon," Sarah uses it as a pretext for 24/7 surveillance that includes moving into Chuck's room. While Sarah lies next to him, pointedly wearing the t-shirt Chuck wore the night he brought a bottle of wine and a single rose to her hotel room (only to have the door opened by Bryce Larkin), Chuck wraps himself in the covers like a mummy. Given the hotel scene in Barstow only a few episodes distant, the viewer knows it is not for lack of desire. Next morning, Sarah arises as Miss Upbeat, while Chuck languishes in bed.

Ultimately, Chuck puts the kybosh on Sarah's plan to share an apartment together, a plan that may have involved motives other than simply assuring his protection. Pushed to a point of frustration he cannot handle, Chuck, again seated on the edge of that fountain, informs Sarah he will not be moving in with her, elaborating, "…Having a fake relationship, that's one thing, but living together is…I mean every day being around each other, and, and…and that's why I can't do it. (Pause) I hope you understand." Sarah, looking away from Chuck, assumes a far-away look in her eyes as he speaks, suggesting the dream of a life together she desires, before responding with words dripping with irony and disappointment: "I do." Before he departs, though, Chuck leaves Sarah with an unprecedented vow of his own that makes her head swirl and lips part after he leaves: "…I am going to get this thing out of my head, one day, I will. And when I do I'm going to live the life that I want with the girl that I love." As events unfold, these words will prove no mere cynical manipulation.

CHAPTER 9:

Orion the Hunter

Ancient Greek mythology reveals less of Orion the Hunter than most classical heroes. Despite this, a composite sketch of the relatively few source materials referencing the shadowy figure present a skilled hunter who is blinded before regaining his sight. Treacherously killed at the hands of another, he wanders as a shade in the Underworld, where Odysseus spies him hunting in The Odyssey. Ultimately, Zeus preserves his legacy by elevating him to a constellation in the night sky. Given this biographical outline, it is no wonder that Chuck's father, Stephen Bartowski, answers to the CIA code name of Orion.

In perhaps the most obvious parallel, the elder Bartowski spends the last decade or more of his life hunting for his wife, code name Frost, after she disappears. To do so, however, Stephen pointedly creates a technological underworld located in the basement of the home where Chuck and Ellie grew up. Amongst a variety of "lasers and gadgets" that make Morgan's eyes pop (vs. the Anniversary), row after row of shelves cram themselves with labeled boxes, many of them filled with documents linked to Orion's global search for his beloved. Further underscoring the underworld and treachery links, Stephen dies at the hands of a traitorous Shaw in the bowels of the Los Angeles subway system.

Deeper digging uncovers the more subtle links between the two Orions. Stephen also suffers a metaphorical blindness from which he is delivered on at least two counts. The opening scene of "vs. the Living Dead" foregrounds him sharpening the blade of an axe in his remote mountain hideout, implying the axe he has to grind with the CIA and its line of work that has so drastically affected his family's life in the past and still may in the future. Upon discovering that Chuck has been lying to him about his return to spying in Season 3, his dad makes it his mission to convince him to get out. A prime opportunity arises when the Castle team opens Shaw's spy will and assumes he is dead. Interjecting himself into the conversation, Stephen preaches, "For every spy, there's somebody that cares for them. Somebody who has to open that box, read that message, and mourn their loss. This is a bad business. And I don't want my family having any part of it." Later, when he tricks Chuck into revealing that he is not just a part-time analyst but has indeed downloaded the Intersect 2.0, Stephen flees, stating, "I'm sorry; I can't stay here and watch my son die." This departure leads Chuck to lament, "He doesn't know anything about me. Why I became the Intersect. That, that I can help people. That for the first time in my life what I do actually means something."

Subsequent events help to cure the elder Bartowski of his blindness in this regard. When Ellie is tricked into bugging her father and Fulcrum converges on his remote cabin, Stephen is vividly shown just how invaluable spies can be in time of need when Chuck and Sarah fortuitously show up on his doorstep. While father and son find themselves bound and on the verge of death inside the cabin, Chuck informs Stephen, "…I came up here to tell you why I wanted to download the Intersect, that I'm special and I can help people, but given the circumstances, I think I'm going to just have to show you." Chuck begins taking out the bad guys in camouflage, and, in a twist of irony, Sarah's timely arrival allows her to throw the very same axe Stephen grinds at the beginning of the episode and deflect a deadly knife, saving Chuck.

After the blinders come off, the transformation in Stephen's attitude is almost immediate. In the next scene back in Echo Park, Orion enters Chuck's room and actually commits to aiding Chuck in his spy life by developing the Governor for his version of the Intersect, explaining, "You're my son. And you downloaded the 2.0 for the same reason I created the original: to help people. You want to be a spy. I'm going to do everything I can to…help you be the man you want to be." With an emotional swallow worthy of Sarah, Chuck steps forward and hugs his new ally.

Chuck helps his dad gain insight on another matter as well. While Chuck languishes in a CIA headquarters detention cell for stabbing Shaw in a misguided attempt to expose him as an Intersect, Stephen succeeds in unlocking Chuck's cell and guiding him out of the building (vs. the Subway). Just as Chuck is about to jump into the Jeep and run with Stephen, Sarah catches up with him and pleads for Chuck to stay, advising him of the burn notice he will face. However, Stephen also pleads with his son: "If you stay, everyone you love will be in danger. You have to choose who you want to protect: you or her?...You have to run to protect her!" Chuck chooses Sarah, and initially leaves with his dad, but circumstances change.

When Morgan informs Chuck that Sarah and Casey have been taken into custody, Chuck tells his dad they must go back. Stephen argues that it's just a trap, claiming they really want Chuck, and ends with another plea of his own: "I'm your father. Do not ask me, please do not ask me to put my own son in jeopardy." Chuck counters, though, ironically citing his father as his inspiration: "Why did you come back this time? You came back because you wanted to protect Ellie and me. Because you knew no matter how far you ran you would never be able to live with yourself if something happened to somebody that you loved." Confronted with truth he cannot deny, Stephen literally makes a U-turn, vowing to work together with Chuck in his quest.

And what about that legacy? Stephen Bartowski may not illuminate the sky each evening after his subway murder, but he leaves two admiring children to continue his life missions and enables them to succeed in his absence using the resources he gave them. Through programming wizardry, even after he is dead, Orion turns the mission to find his wife over to Chuck, giving him the higher purpose to leave the CIA in Season 4 and dedicate himself to the search for and rediscovery of his mother (vs. the Ring: Part II). In addition, Orion leaves a mission to Ellie in the form of the computer he arranges for her to discover (vs. Phase Three). Not only does it store his Intersect research data, but it also enables Chuck to download the Intersect again in Season 4 after his mother suppresses it. Moreover, Ellie's work on that project for the balance of the series brings her fully into Team Bartowski in a significant manner that allows her to use and build upon her own analytic talents (see Chapter 17: Missing Links).

Speaking of discoveries, realizing the lasting greatness of his father is a process that begins for Chuck in Season 2. While handling some of Sarah's baggage regarding her father in "vs. the DeLorean," Chuck commiserates with Sarah by describing his own delinquent dad as "an unusual man," before qualifying, "I guess that's generous." And when Sarah leads Chuck to his father's desert trailer in "vs. the Broken Heart," Chuck interprets his father's concern about leaving before dark as baseless paranoia. Things don't get much better when, upon reaching Echo Park (vs. the Dream Job), the elder Bartowski claims he is not only responsible for Roark Industries' most notable advancements but that they were stolen from him by the famed CEO himself. Even when Stephen secretly leaves the map of the Roark plant on Chuck's bed in a manner that Chuck can link them to the schematics already provided by 'Orion,' Chuck does not have eyes to see his dad as anything more than an eccentric quack.

This attitude changes during a night of epiphanies when Chuck takes on his solo mission to raid Roark Industries and discovers just how brilliant and 'complicated' his father really is (vs. the Dream Job). After 'saving' his irate, seemingly misguided dad from security personnel, Chuck ironically tells him, "I'm not who you think I am." But when Roark's right hand man shows up and tells them it's good to see them both again, the wheels start turning in Chuck's head. With perfect symmetry and timing, Stephen turns to his son and admits, "I'm not who you think I am either." After his fingers dance over a few buttons on his high-tech wrist sleeve, Stephen manages to distract and incapacitate the assailant in the doors, and with a final kick leaves him neutralized. When Chuck subsequently fingers him as Orion, Stephen simply shrugs his shoulders and leads the way to the Intersect room while Chuck still struggles to grasp the fact that his own father is the mythologized CIA legend who invented the Intersect.

But the revelations just keep coming. Stephen confesses he never imagined the Intersect would find Chuck, and links that discovery to arranging his re-entry into Chuck's life: "That's why I came back. That's why I let your handlers find me." But Chuck still has questions that he ends up answering himself:

> **Chuck:** You wanted me to flash on your crazy schematics. You wanted me to break in here. Why didn't you just say who you were?
>
> **Orion:** Would you have trusted me? After not seeing me for ten years and bring you to RI and tell you that I can get the

Intersect, ...which I also built, out of your head, what would you have said to that?

Chuck: That you were a little bit crazy.

Moments later, in the Intersect room, their mutual epiphanies are figured as father and son sit facing one another. Just as the Intersect cube pointedly rotates between them, their perspectives toward and relationship with one another turn upon realizing the other's Intersect-centered identity. Likewise, the glass screens through which they view each other indicate the new transparency they share. However, Chuck also wants his sister to know their father's true identity after his death when they debate in the car whether Chuck should go after Shaw. When Ellie still calls their father "crazy," Chuck is quick to correct her: "He wasn't crazy. Our dad was a hero. He was a great man…who did amazing things. He was not perfect, not as a dad, no. But he was great....And that is the secret I most wanted you to know."

The veil is ultimately drawn away from Chuck's eyes regarding his father's love for his family, too. With the revelation of his father as Orion comes the realization that his father's abandonment of the family was caused primarily by his desire to protect it. As Orion himself says, "I knew I had to stay away from you and your sister." Chuck comes to understand this in "vs. The Ring: Part II" when he leaves Sarah on the curb and flees with his dad to allegedly protect her. And when circumstances change those plans, Chuck uses his knowledge of why his father re-entered the lives of his children—to protect them—as the basis for his decision to return for Sarah.

But Chuck's interaction with Stephen assures him of his father's particular love for him as his son as well. In Season 2, Orion returned to remove the Intersect from Chuck's brain, acknowledging, "It must be such a curse to have all those secrets trapped in your head" (vs. the Dream Job). When he resurfaces at the end of Season 3 (vs. the Living Dead), he shadows Chuck and Sarah on the 'date' to Shaw's loft so he is there to offer a saving hand when Chuck clings to the edge of the building. And after realizing Chuck's mind is disintegrating due to the effects of the Intersect 2.0, he makes it his primary mission to manufacture the Governor to safeguard his sanity and even his life. In the end, Chuck's dad serves as his cheerleader alongside Sarah, always quick to compliment him with his signature "Aces, Charles" or his dying words, "Remember you're special, Son" (vs. the Ring: Part Two).

Those words, recalled in the darkest moments of his short-circuiting Intersect match with Shaw in the Buy More, are responsible for rebooting Chuck and enabling him to overcome his arch rival. Perhaps this pride in his son was Orion's most significant legacy, for in Season 4 it also helps an Intersect-less Chuck persevere in his quest to vanquish Alexei Volkoff. Shrewdly using not only Volkoff's jealousy over Frost but also a virus that his father created, Chuck succeeds in transferring the entire Hydra network on to the cabin computer before Volkoff's arrest by Beckman. Poignantly, Chuck lays his feat at the feet of his father with an illuminating tribute to Volkoff's Bane: "…In the end, it was Stephen J. Bartowski that took you down. Fitting, don't you think? …I am my father's son…" (vs. the Push Mix).

CHAPTER 10:

Tug of War

"It's over, Chuck. You're free, Son."

Soon after Orion, aka Stephen Bartowski, speaks these words in "vs. the Colonel," a bomb explodes in the desert background between Chuck and Sarah during the mop up of Roark's men. Similarly, the climactic removal of the Intersect 1.0 from Chuck's brain rocks not only Chuck's world but also Sarah's, whose wide-eyed expression while sitting beside him in the streaking getaway car betrays the fiery impact of the news. With the invisible barrier of the handler-asset dynamic blown up, the moment of truth regarding the nature and future of their relationship finally arrives. And the tug of war begins.

Initially, all seems on track to their destination: a real couple in the normal world. Sarah arrives for the wedding rehearsal dinner the next evening looking as "amazing" as the promise of their future and asks Chuck how he feels. Reflecting for a moment, Chuck replies, "Feels great, actually…like everything is finally real." Sarah nods and looks into the distance for a moment before concurring, "It is real." After sharing a genuine smile, Chuck caresses her wrist as his hand slides down to take hers. But exactly how real is it?

Next morning in Castle, the briefing with Beckman and its aftermath cast doubt. When the general offers Chuck an analyst position, she urges, "Your government is calling you, Mr. Bartowski." It comes as no surprise that Chuck declines, with humor at that: "Well, then, I think my country might have the wrong number, 'cuz I'm just Chuck Bartowski, not a hero." Anyone who has been listening for the last two seasons knows Chuck's incessant dream has been to retrieve his old, real life. Especially Sarah. Still, the camera captures her silent disappointment, but it soon turns to Sarah's more visible conflict after Chuck leaves to pick up his severance check.

In a seeming derailment of their admittedly ambiguous plans for the future, Sarah accepts Beckman's assignment to head up the new Intersect project and board a flight to Europe in the morning. Just as her surprise partner for the project, Bryce Larkin, reappears, so does Sarah's fear of leaving the spy realm, the only world she has known. Bryce acts as if Sarah's imminent departure from Burbank matches her desires, commenting, "Finally, you can get out of here," but the sentiment is clearly inaccurate. Sarah does not engage Bryce for the first several moments and even then only in a perfunctory manner; visibly shocked, her lips tremble, unable to find words as she contemplates the prospect of moving on both with and without Chuck. Was she a dreamer in more ways than one, thinking herself more capable of making the choice with which she is now faced? Or had she convinced herself Chuck would make a different choice?

Thus begins the first round of tug of war between Chuck and Sarah at the church prior to Ellie's wedding. After pointedly asking Chuck if he has brought the rings, again foregrounding Sarah's future dream of family and a normal life, Sarah appears burdened as she tentatively caresses Chuck's lapel. "You look like a real spy," she claims, while Chuck counters, "You look like a real bridesmaid." Both attempt to identify the other as someone who will fit into their competing worlds: the spy world of Sarah and the normal world of Chuck. And now that the real possibility exists for both to live in either one, each proves intent on pulling the other into the one in which they find comfort.

But Sarah gets cold feet, even though it isn't her wedding. She tries to tell Chuck of her plans, but, impatient to get on with his dream after such delay, he insists on teasing her with a proposal…to take a vacation. Sarah, however, delivers the punch line: "Chuck, I'm leaving in the morning," with Bryce no less. Reality crashes down on Chuck, and it's not the reality he had envisioned. Summoning every ounce of control he can muster, Chuck mutes his devastation and disillusionment before promptly absenting himself: "Thank you for coming to the wedding…It's good for the cover." So the relationship wasn't real after all?

Though Chuck just wants a normal life, the episode proceeds to portray him as anything but normal. After the scheduled wedding dissolves in the wake of a special forces firefight and fire sprinklers,

Sarah, curiously, stops in to check on Chuck at home. She's not quite ready to board that flight. When she asks Chuck if he's OK, he makes clear he is not. Remaining silent on his disappointment with Sarah, Chuck agonizes over his inability to enjoy a life not compromised by his spy life…even when he is no longer a spy, adding, "I just want to be a normal guy who helps his sister in normal ways." Then, spotting his severance check, he realizes how he can do just that…with the help of some friends. When asked if she has time for "one more mission" before leaving, Sarah smirks, impressed once more with Ellie's brother, and comments, "That's not what a normal guy would do."

This observation, and the security it may provide for Sarah's insecurities, signals the beginning of a larger clarification. Indeed, the impromptu wedding on the beach once again figures the central conflict in Sarah's mind, pitting the detachment of the spy life against the fellowship of the normal life…and the fear that she battles to make the leap of faith from one world to the other. While standing as a bridesmaid, participating in the act of uniting man and wife, Sarah observes the stark contrast of Bryce Larkin, a remote spectator, hidden behind a wall of sand in the distance and able to communicate only through the artificiality of an earpiece. Her eyes shift to the ring bearer, joy filling his face as he escorts his beaming sister down the aisle with their redeemed father. Pointedly positioned via camera angle in the distance between Awesome and Ellie, Sarah absorbs the vows they exchange. Meanwhile, the repeated refrain from Slow Club's "Christmas TV" accents the imagery on the screen: "So come on home, just come on home / Just come on home, just come on home." When the voice in her ear asks, "Sarah, you're not coming with me, are you?" the answer from the one who doesn't like to talk is a simple shake of the head. This time, the voice, yet another personification of the fear she has battled since the shower scene in "vs. the Wookiee," is vanquished by a renewed faith in the reality of family and home…and a man who is anything but normal. Sarah inhales, meets Chuck's eyes, and smiles serenely.

But Chuck can't read Sarah's mind. Though she and Bryce know otherwise, Chuck reaches the courtyard wedding reception under the impression this will be his last dance. This time Sarah plays the role of spectator, not entirely remote like Bryce at the wedding, but pointedly watching the festivities from the edges with a wistful expression, a wall flower hesitant to join in. Chuck approaches and stands behind her, looking at events from what he perceives as her point of view. Inquiring about Bryce, Chuck assumes they will soon be leaving to "save the world." But Sarah redirects rather than confirms. She wishes to keep her secret a moment longer, long enough to probe Chuck's heart one last time.

In asking Chuck to dance, to leave the periphery for the center of the courtyard, Sarah signals that she is prepared to enter the normal world with Chuck as her partner by her side. But as they dance silently, her chin resting on his shoulder, Sarah prepares one last time to pull Chuck into her world before she must leave hers for his. Chuck starts this second round of tug of war, ironically, by supporting Sarah's decision: "You belong out there, saving the world. Just…just I'm not that guy." With an intimacy that also ironizes the distant, artificial voice of Bryce at the wedding, she whispers into Chuck's ear what she has been telling him for two years: "How many times do you have to be a hero to realize that you are that guy?" But Chuck pulls back: "…I want more, Sarah. I want a life. I want a real life." With Chuck's position entrenched, Sarah, letting go of the rope, steps back and gazes into his eyes. Finally resolved, as in "vs. the Santa Claus," to pull the trigger--but this time without the bloodshed or moral ambiguity--Sarah begins, "Chuck, I don't want to save the world… I want…."

But she never finishes her sentence. Orion's flash doesn't let her. In another flash, Sarah is gone to save Bryce, and Chuck is left trying to grasp his own future reality without Sarah. Watching her leave without him leads to his own epiphany: he simply cannot let her go to face the danger alone. When his dad tries to stop him, telling him it's not his job anymore and wanting to protect his own son as Chuck wants to protect Sarah, Chuck confesses to his father the only truth that could make him relent: "Dad, I love her." Following his own advice, given to Morgan just minutes prior, Chuck follows his heart, because his brain "only screw[s] things up." Just as Sarah was prepared to give up her world for Chuck, Chuck is willing to give up his for hers. And circumstances will soon tilt the matter toward the latter. Their mutual sacrifice fulfills Ellie's prophetic words at the start of the episode, when she revealed why she opted for the formal church wedding instead of insisting on the toes-in-the-sand version she ultimately got: "…You make sacrifices for family."

The credits don't roll yet. Chuck has one more epiphany, one that will also change the course of his life…and, indirectly, his relationship with Sarah, at least for a season (make that half a season?). When

Chuck encounters the mortally wounded Bryce Larkin in the Intersect room, he pleads with him to "hold on!" But despite his hopeful words and visions of what Bryce and Sarah will still do together, Bryce's eyes permanently glaze over. With Casey and Sarah either stalled, captured, or dead, suddenly there is no one else left to save the day. Only Chuck. Clearly, the world needs more heroes to step in, but who will stand in the breach now? Tomorrow? Beginning to grasp his responsibility and unique position, Chuck finally confronts his own insecurities. A montage of doubts and validations stream through his mind even as the villains threaten to breach the door. A choice must be made. Significantly, Sarah's words are the last to resonate in his mind: "How many times do you have to be a hero to realize you are that guy?" The time to stay in the car has passed.

With the click of a button, the download of the Intersect begins, and Chuck reenters the spy world. But this time he chooses his destiny. No more self-pity. And it comes with a surprise. After the Ring agents penetrate the white room and discover the destruction of the Intersect, Chuck's decision is revealed. (Casey captures the magnitude of the moment: "Oh, Chuck me!") And so are his kung-fu skills. After taking out the bad guys in a way he never could have imagined, and saving the lives of Casey and Sarah in the process, Chuck is left staring at his hands with amazement and confusion. Similarly, Sarah, shock filling her face, calls out what sounds like a question: "Chuck!?" Alas, it foreshadows the approach of a dark period, one in which both Chuck and Sarah must grapple with exactly who the Intersect 2.0 really is.

CHAPTER 11:

The Man Who Lived in a Wall

Morgan: Man, that dude is creepy.

Chuck: Agreed.

Chuck and Morgan must be at the Nerd Herd desk discussing the latest unfortunate revelation from the lips of Jeff or Lester, right? Or perhaps commenting on any of the dozen shadow-world villains that wander into the Buy More over the first two seasons of the series? Try Casey. After Sarah leaves the fountain at the end of "vs. the Tango" (Season 1, Episode 3), Morgan strolls across the courtyard to a dreamy Chuck only to notice the bulky Buy More green shirt, always ready to sell a Beast Master barbecue by day, peering at them through the window of his apartment that evening, his fingers separating the blinds. If that isn't disturbing enough, viewers learn in Season 4 that Casey spent two weeks living inside the walls of the Costa Gravan premier's estate while stalking him as "The Angel of Death" during an '80s assassination attempt. Of course, these images, along with his name, serve a deeper purpose: figuring Casey's emotional encasement for much of the series. In pointed contrast, Chuck, Mr. Feelings, observes an open-window policy, both literally and figuratively, of which even Casey occasionally takes advantage.

From the outside looking in, Casey seemingly has no feelings. In the pilot, viewers are partially introduced to the NSA major through the wild car chase that nearly gets everyone killed. With stone-cold eyes, Casey stares through the windshield across locked bumpers at Sarah and Chuck while trying to run them off the road. On the helipad, when subsequently confronting Chuck and the "CIA skirt" that he has already given clearance to kill, Casey robotically tries to speed matters along:

"It's late. I'm tired. Let's cut the crap and give him to me now! He belongs to the NSA." And Sarah's staged threat to kill Chuck rather than give him to Casey doesn't stir the slightest hint of concern: "You shoot him, I shoot you, I leave both your bodies here and go out for a late snack. I'm thinking maybe pancakes."

When assigned to Burbank for a longer stint than he envisioned, Casey doesn't get any chummier. On multiple occasions, Casey literally pushes would-be intruders away from him, usually a poor soul trying to make an emotional connection, and they end up sprawling on the ground or among the boxes of the nearest ruined toaster display. Not surprisingly, he pushes others away in a variety of non-literal ways as well. Compared to Sarah, Casey follows a decidedly negative approach to handling the Intersect. As early as Episode 2 in Season 1 (vs. the Helicopter), the first thing Casey chooses to say after a panicked Chuck manages to evade Dr. Zarnow and find his way behind the chopper's controls is to reprimand him: "I thought I told you to stay in the car!" Then when Chuck struggles with the directions given him, Casey adds, "Listen, Moron, do you want to die?!" Within seconds, both Chuck and Sarah insist he hand over the phone, and Sarah's soothing, pretend-you're-playing-a-video-game-at-home approach yields a far better result.

Even when Chuck does succeed, facetiousness proves the NSA handler's preferred handling technique. In fact, Casey so rarely resorts to sincerity early on in the series that when he actually does praise Chuck, "Good work last night," Chuck's knee-jerk response is to ask "very nicely if you would ease up on the sarcasm" (vs. the Tango). Similarly, Casey is all too ready to respond with the back-handed compliment. In Season 2 (vs. the Best Friend), when thinking Chuck is speeding away in the Nerd Herd vehicle to dispose of a bomb, Casey honors him with the moniker of "imbecilic hero." When not belittling Chuck, Casey expresses his general displeasure through non-verbal expressions like his constantly gritted teeth or signature grunt. Sarah perhaps best describes Casey in "vs. the Sensei" as "combat ready at all times," explaining, "Casey is always mad. That's his base line." In the same episode, Sarah counters Casey's probing of her feelings for Chuck by ironically pointing out, "All I'll admit to is having feelings."

Unlike Sarah, whose emotional walls prove the residue of a difficult and isolated childhood, Casey's walls are largely self-imposed to enable him to pursue a greater, principled dream. On a dark night in the Honduran jungle (vs. the Tic Tac), Colonel Keller presents the young lieutenant with the biggest choice of his life: "Either you go home to your family, or you become the soldier you always dreamed you could be. So tell me, Lt. Coburn, are you ready to die today?" Indeed, joining the covert black ops team requires his death as Alex Coburn and resurrection as John Casey, assassin and marksman noncom pare. The only wrinkle is that he has a fiancé waiting for him at home.

As he tells Chuck twenty years later, "I made my decision between love and love of country a long time ago, and it was the right decision for me." In his apartment a season earlier (vs. the Undercover Lover), Casey reflects, "It's not like I want the kids and the van and the Little League practices and the Costco run." His pay-off? The satisfaction of protecting "the greater good," the American Dream: "I do what I do so all the other slobs can have it." Ironically, the same basic sentiment evidences itself in the pilot's helipad scene when he tells the wide-eyed Chuck, "Look, we're the good guys. We get paid to keep bombs from exploding." On a more comic level, Casey also pursues his dream car, the fortress-like Crown Vic that further figures its owner. Casey cares for it meticulously like his own child. In this case, investing his emotions in a static material item safeguards his feelings…that is until it is blown up by a guided missile!

Pursuing his patriotic dream of the greater good also means living by another principle: loyalty to regulations and the chain of command. His decision made, Casey abides by the rules, and he bristles when others do not. Concerned that Sarah is breaking protocol with the asset due to the emotional connection she forms with Chuck, Casey finds himself compelled to confront Sarah over whether she has compromised herself with the Intersect (vs. the Crown Vic). Waxing philosophic, Casey lectures Sarah, "The choice we made to protect something bigger than ourselves is the right choice. As hard as that is for you to remember sometimes."

The Sarah of late Season 5, jaded with amnesia, also speaks to this trait. When Casey stops by the hotel room to drop off the video log, he asks Sarah to describe his reputation prior to meeting her five years prior. Notably, she describes him as "unquestioning about your orders." Never is this more evident when instructed by Beckman to eliminate Chuck in "vs. the First Date" on the eve of the new Intersect coming online. Though he is clearly conflicted over this assignment and even attempts to suggest an alternative, he seems prepared to follow through if necessary.

As Casey's response to the kill order on Chuck reveals, Casey does have feelings despite his self-imposed walls; he just hunkers down behind them to cope. These emotions reveal themselves late in Season 1 during "vs. the Undercover Lover," which presents his past relationship with Ilsa Trinchina, who he thinks died in a bomb blast in Chechnya. Flashing on her name on a hotel guest list, Chuck discovers Casey's hidden past as her "Sugar Bear." When Chuck ill-advisedly teases Casey with the nickname, as Casey would surely do in Chuck's position, Casey almost strangles him. Still, Chuck becomes so frustrated with Casey's subsequent inability to admit his interest in Ilsa that he calls his handler a "freaking robot." This exasperation cracks Casey's defenses, and he finally spills the details with pained voice and drawn face, beginning, "She was the most beautiful thing I'd ever seen." When he encounters Ilsa again in a Los Angeles hotel during the mission, he comes undone, standing transfixed and speechless. After discovering she intends to marry a Russian mobster, Casey proceeds to drown his sorrows alone in his apartment.

Similarly, Casey displays his vulnerability in Season 2 when he discovers that his former mentor, Ty Bennett, has turned traitor and attempts to recruit Casey for The Ring (vs. the Sensei). Despite his mockery of Chuck's "lady feelings" when the Intersect initially admits he'd like some time to sort things out in the wake of the Jill arc, it is Casey who struggles to control his feelings in "vs. the Sensei." Sarah reassures Chuck that Casey's pitch to bench the Intersect for the mission is not about Chuck but his betrayal by Bennett, explaining, "When you have a mentor like that, a real trust develops between you, and Casey feels betrayed." Indeed, his formerly beloved bonsai tree, a link to Bennett, soon finds its unceremonious way into the trash can. In fact, Casey becomes so "emotionally involved" that later he not only endangers the asset when Chuck is locked in a car trunk but even angrily projects his feelings of betrayal on to Sarah when she tells him that Beckman is right to bench him because he is too "emotionally involved," claiming, "20 years in the business has taught me one sure thing: that people, people let you down in the end."

Perhaps the most vivid evidence of Casey's carefully guarded emotions is found in his willingness to commit treason and risk the very patriotic dream for which he has sacrificed so much for the higher principle of preserving his former fiancé's safety, even though she doesn't even know he is still alive. When he receives the threat from his former commander, Colonel Keller, to cooperate with the Ring or consider Kathleen a dead woman, Casey steals the Laudanol from a CIA holding facility. In doing so, he notably proves unable to follow Keller's advice from the past. Moments before killing Keller, his former superior admonishes his one-time protégé: "You know you wouldn't be in this mess if you'd done what I told you 20 years ago. You were supposed to let go of her. Stop caring." Casey simply couldn't.

Casey gains a tad more balance as his emotional walls shrink under the tutelage of an unlikely sensei, Chuck. Sarah herself honors Chuck with this title at the end of "vs. the Sensei" when congratulating him after he correctly advises Casey to forsake calm and channel his inner beast, enabling him to defeat Bennett in the dojo. Earlier in the episode, with Sarah's help, Chuck realizes, "If I were really a friend, I would look past what he's saying and remember how he's feeling." Chuck followed the same policy in Season 1 when encouraging Casey to follow his heart and pursue Ilsa. Though his efforts initially result in having his mouth sealed courtesy of a bar code gun, Chuck eventually succeeds in convincing Casey. This starts innocuously enough, getting Casey to watch hotel monitors, heats up when urging Casey to meet the solitary bride in the bar lounge, and almost climaxes with a tryst in her hotel room interrupted by her drunk husband-to-be. Later, when Casey thinks a bug they discover has betrayed her real identity as a French spy, he ends up plunging several stories into the pool (with Chuck literally bound by his side) in an effort to foil the 'marriage' to the mobster. Ultimately, he does reconnect with Ilsa before she must disappear once more into the shadows. Fighting sentimentality, Casey tells Chuck, "A spy's life."

These specific examples of Chuck's growing influence over Casey point to his larger, more general effect on Casey's growth. Over the first two and a half seasons, Casey's loyalty evolves to a point not so narrowly defined. As he becomes closer with his formerly disparaged partners, he makes exceptions and places government priorities behind friends in time of need. In one step in this process, Casey seems touched by Sarah's referring to him as her "partner" while under the truth serum in "vs. the Truth." And after Chuck and Sarah team up to help him with Ilsa and Bennett, Casey reverses himself in "vs. the Colonel" to join up with the temporarily rogue spies to help them find Orion.

This cycle continues when Chuck and Sarah again risk their careers and prison time to help him in "vs. the Tic Tac" by ambushing Keller's men and guarding Kathleen, respectively. In the very next episode, Casey returns the favor by proactively serving as a substitute to kill the mole in Chuck's Red Test (vs. the Final Examination). But Casey also proceeds to atone for the guilt he acquired on his treasonous "vs. the Tic Tac" mission. Chuck places his faith in Casey by asking him to join the rogue mission to Paris, where Casey apprehends the Ring Director and thereby gains his reinstatement to the CIA. Thus, over time, Casey slowly integrates into Team/Family Bartowski, accepting invitations to parties and even Thanksgiving dinner. Though still a work in progress, Casey is far better prepared to grapple with perhaps his most formidable emotional challenge looming ahead when, even as he succeeds in protecting his former fiancé, he discovers he is a father (see Chapter 15: Wall Comes Tumbling Down).

CHAPTER **12:**

Wandering Into the Promised Land

Echo Park. As the name implies, the events that transpire in Chuck's Los Angeles neighborhood have a way of repeating themselves, if with slight variations. On a structural level, the name also hints at "Chuck's" distinct echoing of a classic text. Indeed, when viewed within the framework of literary form, the first two and a half seasons notably reprise elements of the Old Testament as they figuratively stage Chuck and Sarah's relationship as an epic, detour-prone journey that ultimately reaches a Promised Land.

For the bulk of Seasons 1 and 2, Chuck and Sarah languish in an Egyptian captivity of sorts, the invisible prison of handler/asset protocol. Specifically, most of Season 1 is spent determining if their cover relationship also has a basis in reality, but neither Chuck nor Sarah is able to know for certain until Sarah is no longer duty-bound to protect Chuck and motivate him to perform. Even once the events of "vs. First Date" confirm the fact that their cover relationship does indeed have a real foundation, the relationship is largely put on hold again when the destruction of the new Intersect computer requires the resumption of their professional relationship. Handcuffed in their ability to fully investigate their feelings for one another and uncertain about what the future holds, the focus increasingly turns to the question of what decisions each will make if and when the Intersect is finally removed from Chuck's brain.

The Castle couple's relational incarceration is followed, notably, by a rushed nocturnal escape to the desert (vs. the First Kill), the modern Sinai of Barstow. When Sarah chooses to go rogue rather than betray Chuck and her own dream of a real life to a D. C. bunker, they are finally free to follow their hearts to their natural destination. Chuck and Sarah take little more than a day to come within a Morgan-borrowed condom of consummating their clearly still-genuine feelings for each other after a passionate hotel awakening (vs. the Colonel). All signs indicate that Chuck and Sarah, both affirming what they share is "real," are on the verge of finally entering their own Promised Land, even if it requires Sarah to put saving the world on hold (see Chapter 10: Tug of War). That is until Chuck downloads the Intersect 2.0 while answering the call of duty to fill the breach in time of need. Staring at his newly-lethal hands, Chuck seems just as confused regarding his identity at the close of Season 2 as Sarah, who calls out his name across the Intersect room more as a question than a celebration: "Chuck?!"

This foreshadowing comes to an ironic fruition at the opening of Season 3. In almost 12 full episodes of the following arc, Chuck and Sarah's relationship and respective senses of self ultimately digress into such incoherence that wandering in a desert wilderness serves as an apt metaphor even if it only seems like forty years. The first half of this segment (roughly Episodes 1-6) focuses on their emotional straying from one another. Chuck kick-starts this dynamic in "vs. the Pink Slip" when, in a complete reversal of the first two seasons, he chooses pursuing life as a spy in the Prague train station over the unencumbered life Sarah offers and for which he has dreamed so long (more on this below). No one is more shocked and devastated by the revelation than Sarah, whose newfound skepticism regarding the spy life also proves a reversal from Season 2. So after Chuck fails out of the spy school specifically created for him, and returns to Burbank as a Forrest Gump look-alike (in his beard stage) to salve his pain with jumbo jars of cheeseballs, he must still endure the wrath of a scorned woman who prefers to throw her cell phone into a pool rather than answer his calls.

Indeed, Chuck experiences a slap of reality, both literally and figuratively, during his unwelcome insertion into Sarah's delicate mission upon her return to Burbank, compromising it if not for Sarah's improvised outrage. Sarah's continued vengefulness leads even Casey to comment, "...I've seen men have their fingernails pulled off more humanely that you treated that kid," adding over Sarah's protests, "Put him out of his misery. He deserves that much." When her first attempt to "say a proper goodbye" is interrupted by another mission detour, Sarah finally concludes their conversation at the end of Episode 1. But even after Chuck outlines his altruistic motives for his action in Prague, Sarah assures him, "I..acted impulsively, and it's a mistake I don't usually make.

And it won't happen again." And when Chuck tries to bend the conversation back to them, Sarah interrupts to leave no doubt: "You're a spy now, Chuck. You have to keep your feelings to yourself." Sarah doubles down in the second episode (vs. the Three Words) when sparring with Chuck in Castle. Charged by Beckman to get Chuck functioning, and realizing he must become emotionally hard for his own protection, Sarah fiercely taunts Chuck over his pursuit of the spy-life: "Learn to ignore your emotions. Spies do not have feelings. Feelings get you killed. You need to learn to bury them in a place deep inside." And when he claims he won't fight back because he doesn't want to hurt her, she spews, "Don't worry, Chuck. You can't."

Of course, Sarah's calling her impulse to run with Chuck "a mistake" echoes her words about The Incident with Chuck in Season 1. And just as then, Sarah's reaction betrays the sting of her lingering feelings for Chuck. In the middle of "vs. the Pink Slip," Sarah actually admits, "I was mad…and wrong" when telling Chuck he doesn't "work anymore." However, as in Season 1, Carina provides the most transparent view into Sarah's closely re-guarded heart. While out clubbing with Sarah on her own mission (vs. the Three Words), Carina, astounded at Sarah's claim of a strictly "professional relationship" with Chuck, replies, "Oh my God, Walker!…You're just really into him…." Soon after, Carina finds the charm bracelet, and even though Sarah now claims, "It's not really my thing," the sight of it still sparks Sarah to ask, "Do you ever wonder about a different life?" that includes getting ready for a real engagement party. Carina even informs the neurotic Chuck of Sarah's hidden mindset so his hurt feelings will stop sabotaging her mission: "You idiot! The reason Sarah is so cold is because she loves you." Indeed, consciously or unconsciously, Chuck's captivation by the spy life remains on Sarah's mind, as she cryptically implies to Chuck through the wall of the Mexican jail cell: "I need you to break out of your cell and come and get me. I couldn't pick the stupid lock" (vs. the Pink Slip).

For a while, it appears their desert wandering may lead to an oasis. After an initial venting, Sarah mellows enough to call a truce by the end of "vs. the Three Words." While Chuck is cleaning up the debris from the courtyard party the night before, Sarah abruptly approaches Chuck while on her way home to inform him, "I'm listening if there's something you want to say." Contrary to Chuck's cynical assumption, she claims, "I'm good here…for now," suggesting a path to reconciliation before pointing out that his emotions, even though they still prevent him from flashing, were critical in talking Carina's mark down when on the verge of killing her. Looking around the courtyard, Sarah further notes, "It's quite a mess we made," but she speaks metaphorically. Picking up the theme, Chuck replies, "I'm hoping we can clean it up, though." "Maybe," Sarah offers, accepting the white flag, "But you're on your own with the courtyard." These words find more expression when Carina drops off the flash drive from the just-concluded mission recording Chuck's barely-conscious ramblings while locked in the safe room. In the space and privacy of a vacant Castle, Sarah not only finds herself able to listen to Chuck's reasoning for pursuing life as a spy rather than running with her but becomes visibly moved by his declaration of love for her.

The relationship picks up increased momentum as Chuck and Sarah move beyond a truce to reestablish a friendship. In Episode 3 (vs. the Angel Del Muerte), their feelings for one another resurface while escorting Awesome and Ellie to Costa Grava in order to protect the life of Premier Goya. While doing so, they engage in mirror conversations, Chuck with Awesome and Sarah with Ellie. Each spouse appears incredulous that Chuck and Sarah claim to no have no feelings for the other even as they make frequent eye contact across the hall. Ellie particularly challenges Sarah, "Look at yourself right now…Look me in the eye and tell me that you guys are just friends," before confiding to her the "hot and cold patches" she and Devon experience. Sarah remains silent but listens attentively. And when Casey finds himself in serious trouble during the mission, Chuck and Sarah unite to save him, working comfortably and effectively together. By episode's end, when Chuck asks Sarah what she thinks their cover should be going forward, she suggests, "…How about friends?" They even find the grace to cautiously compliment one another: while Chuck admits, "I suppose I could fake being friends with someone like you," Sarah confesses, "And I don't find you completely… repulsive…."

Though she's not quite ready to hang out and play videos, Sarah is game for group gatherings. By the end of Episode 4 (vs. Operation Awesome), Sarah is once again a guest at a Bartowski dinner party and "glad" to be there, her eyes meeting Chuck's across the room. And at work inside Castle, Sarah becomes Chuck's defender against a seemingly misguided new boss, Shaw. When Shaw claims, "Family and friends make us vulnerable," putting "everyone in even greater danger," Sarah counters, "Sometimes it helps to know you've got something to lose" and locks eyes again with Chuck. Similarly, in Episode 5 (vs. First Class), Sarah evidences angst over her perception of Shaw's recklessness in sending Chuck on a mission she feels he is not prepared for and even pleads with Chuck not to go. When he manages to survive, she closes her eyes in tangible relief. Things become so relaxed between the two that Sarah seems pleased to resume touching Chuck's person while helping put in the earpiece for his mission handling Manoosh (vs. the Nacho Sampler), returning the dynamic to the natural chemistry of Seasons 1 and 2. And when Chuck proceeds to ask Sarah about her own experience when first making contact with him at the Nerd Herd desk, Sarah, smiling brightly, waxes nostalgic. Though Chuck recalls himself as "pathetic," Sarah firmly disagrees: "No! You were sweet and innocent. I liked you. That made it much harder." Alas, this proves a high water mark. Just as the viewer begins to expect their relationship may blossom once again, the roots begin to dry up in their desert wandering.

In Episodes 5 and 4, the arrival of two third parties, Hannah and Shaw, respectively, begins this process. Over the next several episodes, Chuck and Sarah reverse course and eventually drift apart again into competing relationships for the first time since "vs. the Santa Claus," when, kneeling before one another, they promised a mutual devotion to their "real" relationship (see Chapter 7: Thunder and Rain). This massive shift climaxes in Episode 7, which pointedly features a golden calf--make that mask--on loan from a Middle Eastern museum no less (vs. the Mask). And just as both Sarah and Chuck plunge head-first into the vault while retrieving the ancient artifact, the events of the day not only plunge both into separate, idolatrous relationships but also into a psychological pit that inverts their lives.

It all begins innocently enough, with Hannah, out of a job, following Chuck to Burbank after meeting him on the flight involving Chuck's solo mission. Telling Chuck he's "different" and "stand[s] out," Hannah confesses losing her job "almost makes it worth it" to gain close proximity as a fellow Nerd Herder (vs. First Class). Chuck proves hungry for her affection given, as subtly figured in the scene stealing the mask, that Sarah has kept him hanging while she fights her own internal battles. Accordingly, Chuck finds it difficult to resist Hannah's amorous advances despite his prior experience with Lou in Season 1, when he supposedly realized the problematic nature of conducting a necessarily deceptive relationship with a civilian. However, the temptation becomes too strong when Hannah makes a pass at him in the control room at the museum (vs. the Mask). And when Hannah, seeing Sarah on the surveillance screen, asks Chuck whether his relationship with Sarah is over, Chuck disingenuously replies, "100% Donezo."

Meanwhile, Sarah quietly notes the emergence of the new relationship. When she arrives at the Buy More to retrieve Chuck and save the suffocating Shaw in the mask vault, she gains a good view of Chuck and Hannah's flirtatious conversation, and surely the surveillance feed from the Buy More provides additional opportunities. Thus, when Hannah is slated for inclusion on the mask mission, Sarah surreptitiously questions the merits of involving a civilian. Still, after Shaw elicits a decidedly negative response from kissing her neck on the mission, Sarah appears initially relieved if not in fact glad to pair up with her old "partner" when Chuck must step in for Shaw to prevent his identification by a Ring operative.

Within this context, and pointedly directly above the idolatrous mask they attempt to steal, Chuck and Sarah engage in a jealous lover's quarrel recalling the one about Lou in the car trunk in "vs. the Imported Hard Salami." Chuck, who has just been on the receiving end of the pass from Hannah, ironically confronts Sarah on Shaw's inability to "keep his hands off" Sarah during the mission while also noting Shaw's flirtatious delivery of coffee each morning. Sarah, in turn, calls Chuck out on his hypocrisy, claiming Hannah can't keep her hands off Chuck. Moreover, she exposes Chuck's lie about the status of his relationship with Hannah, noting, "I didn't realize professional meant having her perfume lathered all over you." From there, circumstances and a strange mix of insecurity/ pride create an intoxicating brew that induces Chuck and Sarah to continue masking their feelings for one another (thus the title of the episode) and redirecting their idolatry away from one another to others.

Though Sarah hides the depth of her disappointment, Chuck's romantic involvement with Hannah, combined with her perception of changes occurring within him (see below), leaves Sarah in crisis. Nothing else can explain the dramatic reversal of her relationship with Shaw that materializes following her quarrel with a perfumed Chuck. To say nothing of the constant stream of negative and even hostile signals she sends Shaw in earlier episodes, Sarah privately drops a swizzle stick Shaw brings in the trash, disdainfully informs Shaw they "definitely have not slept together" when required to confirm their cover, and even claims Shaw is "embarrassing [them] both" in violating "professional boundaries" in "vs. the Mask" alone. Yet, in the very same episode Sarah responds positively to Shaw's confession that he was "hitting" on her with a smirking confession of her own while locked down in a contaminated Castle. In fact, she actually claims to have liked the way he was kissing her neck on the mission, calling her initial, repulsed response an "overreact[ion]." And when Chuck sees Sarah cuddled up to Shaw after he heroically carries her to the museum, it only firms Chuck's resolve to pursue matters with the doe-eyed Hannah, who herself has only narrowly escaped death due to Chuck's heroism.

At the conclusion of the episode, though, Sarah still hesitates on moving ahead with Shaw before clarifying Chuck's level of devotion to Hannah. Following Chuck out as he leaves Castle, Sarah ostensibly wants to make sure he is "OK" with the news he will be trained to work "autonomously" rather than part of the team. This pursuit and outward expression of concern for Chuck is a notable first for Sarah in Season 3. However, Sarah's less obvious purpose of seeking him out privately, echoing Gideon in the Old Testament's Book of Judges, is to put out a fleece to determine whether any feelings for her still linger within Chuck and should hold her back.

This dynamic becomes evident when she cautiously shifts the conversation to them in a self-deprecating manner, claiming, "…At some point I'm just going to be standing in your way…and not just professionally." Chuck, uncertain or unable to decipher Sarah's ulterior intentions, hesitates before ironically making Sarah reveal her cards first by asking, "Are you sure you're OK with the whole Hannah thing?" Sarah, not prepared to show her hand in this context, essentially folds. Initially, she responds with a pasted smile and troubled eyes that have difficulty matching her positive words: "Oh, I shouldn't have given you a hard time. She's great, and…." When her words fail and renegade emotions momentarily jump over her interior walls, Sarah is left silently licking her lips, appeal in her eyes. Chuck fills the gap with kind but similarly insincere sentiments: "…You [and Shaw] are perfect together. It's disgusting…in, in a heart-warming kind of way." Despite Chuck's attempt at levity, Sarah's pursed features betray disappointment at his supportive comments. Chuck continues, perhaps more genuinely, to note Shaw's role in saving Sarah from the toxic gas and admits, "…If I have to see you with someone else, it may as well be a hero, right?" His words leave Sarah with no dignified option other than to return his compliment, and that's exactly what she does while displaying, significantly, her most sincere expression of the scene: "What can I say? I have a type." All that is left to be said is a whispered goodbye.

Thus, a strange blend of mutual concern for the other's happiness, Chuck's inability to gauge Sarah's defenses, and a coinciding pride/insecurity that prevents both from revealing their true feelings succeeds in extending their wandering by sealing off their path back to one another. As Chuck walks away, neither appears happy. Indeed, Sarah's eyes follow Chuck's slow, slump-shouldered exit from Castle and her personal life. In the aftermath, Sarah's sigh and distinctly disappointed expression indicates not a nostalgic melancholy over the end of a significant season of her life but rather an earnest sadness that the fleece she too subtly put out doesn't return the desired answer and even firms their separation. Before the evening is over, she'll be submitting to a shoulder rub from Shaw despite chewing nervously on a swizzle stick.

After misreading Sarah, Chuck proceeds with that headlong plunge into his relationship with Hannah. Following a passionate evening in the video room at the Buy More with Chuck, Hannah spends the night, only to meet Ellie while wrapped in a towel the next morning (vs. the Fake Name). In Castle, Casey interprets the ensuing chipper mood of Chuck, who brings powdered sugar donuts, by commenting, "Stallion had a date last night and must of gotten lucky." Sarah's initial expression of amusement quickly transitions to downcast eyes. However, the donuts metaphorically suggest Chuck's relationship with Hannah may be sweet only on the surface and not healthy. And after dinner that evening, ironically cooked by Shaw and Sarah, Hannah offers a heart-felt toast, claiming, "Right at this second I feel that I am right where I'm supposed to be," before reprising the doughnuts by noting, "I hope that dessert doesn't suck."

Alas, it will. Chuck's response to her toast is underwhelming, giving credence to Jeff's remarkable insight voiced at the Buy More earlier that day: "None of [Chuck's other girlfriends] matter. Chuck may try to replace her, but when he is with Sarah, the light in his eyes shines brightly." In this context, Chuck's switching the fake mask for the real one at the museum takes on added meaning. While posing as an assassin the next day, Chuck has his own tardy epiphany. Eavesdropping on Sarah's conversation with Shaw at his hotel room while pointedly spying through the long-range sniper gun scope, Chuck finally gains the perspective to see Sarah as "my girl, sort a" and displays difficulty staying in character. This begins a tailspin in which he realizes, again, he can't "compartmentalize" his life effectively anymore, including a relationship based on false pretenses with a woman who doesn't really know about his spy life. Before the day is over, a tearful Chuck seeks out Ellie and agrees with her assessment: "...It feels dishonest because you still have feelings for Sarah. " Chuck, coming to grips with his self-delusion, reverses course and Hannah is history, a ringing rebuke at their parting well-deserved.

While Chuck blindly plunges forward, a struggling Sarah pauses to rethink things with Shaw one more time when reminded of Shaw's aggressive sensuality over lunch (vs. the Fake Name). After Shaw confesses his desire to eat her dessert and notes her "sexy" manner of continuing to impersonally use his last name, Sarah informs him she doesn't think they should see each other "in a non-work capacity," citing a need to "stop mixing my personal life with my professional life." However, it doesn't take Sarah long to succumb to the pain and reverse her "pre-emptive break-up." Soon after hearing Casey's blunt commentary on Chuck's date, Sarah, with mournful longing, watches the surveillance feed in Castle that broadcasts Chuck's family dinner, including Hannah's heart-felt toast. Sarah proves so immersed in the scene that she doesn't even note Shaw's entry until he speaks, startling her, despite his already dropping gear on the table. Quickly gathering herself, she wastes no time clocking out, her face unable to mask her angst. Thus begins Sarah's own free fall that extends beyond the strictly emotional to include an existential dimension pushing her towards the nearest ear.

The tentative, vulnerable and even irrational Sarah that shows up at Shaw's hotel door is unprecedented in the series. Though she nervously asks Shaw, in no hurry to replace his bath towel, to "put on some clothes," she seems attracted despite herself. After dismissing Sarah's apology for the quick exit the night before, Shaw tries to help the tongue-tied blonde find her words by asking if she's OK with "the whole Chuck-Hannah thing." It takes several moments for Sarah to master her wide-eyed expression and vacant voice, but when she does she redirects the conversation to Chuck's alleged transformation. Though Shaw sees it simply as part of becoming a spy, Sarah insists the issue is more significant: "...Lives are being affected here," her use of the third person plural another self-defense mechanism. She goes on to link Chuck's alleged metamorphosis to her own identity crisis, claiming, "It's like I'm watching Chuck disappear, and the further he gets from who he is...the more I want to remember who I am. Who I was before all of this." Desperate for the intimacy that acted as an anchor to her sense of self and a link to the real world with Chuck now out of her life, Sarah desperately shifts the conversation to her most guarded secret, her real name, which she has never told anyone, "not even Chuck." At Shaw's urging, she reveals it to the one she despised only days earlier with a curious smile and then proceeds to accept his kiss. And when Sarah initiates a second kiss with Shaw that evening in Castle, it ironically coincides with Chuck saying goodbye to Hannah.

The psychological wilderness in which Sarah subsequently meanders with Shaw proves so ironic that it fails to cohere with her tenure in Burbank. In one regard, Sarah attempts to replace her intimate yet platonic relationship with Chuck, who repeatedly claims they never slept together, with pursuit of a relationship that foregrounds the sexual, the sensual, and the material. Formerly put off by Shaw's sexual innuendos, even when simply dining and establishing covers, Sarah is soon spending afternoons in Shaw's loft with a man whose library includes The Guide to Getting it On and the Karma Sutra. An episode later in Season 3 (vs. the Living Dead) reveals that Shaw and Sarah spend their time in D.C. enjoying a couple's massage, a gourmet chef's tasting menu, and a trip to Tiffany's, where he buys her diamond ear rings. She even continues to call him by his last name. In a sober moment with Chuck, Sarah herself describes her relationship with Shaw as "different...than with you" (vs. the Final Examination).

Perhaps even more incongruent, Sarah finds herself drawn to a man who already epitomizes the very type of spy Sarah fears Chuck is becoming. Indeed, Shaw applauds his perception of Chuck's development at every turn, whether his emerging talent in lying, impersonating, burning an asset, or killing a mole. Even during Sarah's desperate visit to his hotel room, Shaw affirms the very changes inverting her world by proudly pronouncing, "He's becoming a spy." Moreover, Shaw insists that Chuck not only identify and arrest the mole to achieve his spy certification but kill him. He even requires Sarah's participation, saying, "If you give him the order to kill Perry, he'll do it." And after Shaw thinks Chuck has killed the mole, he 'comforts' a distraught Sarah by supporting Chuck's action, claiming, "Chuck...like the rest of us...did it to serve his country" (vs. the Final Exam).

So does Sarah really believe she will find herself and real intimacy with Shaw? Her actions make so little sense one is left with the distinct impression there is actually some degree of punitive self-loathing or purposeful burying of Sarah's ideal self involved. Indeed, Sarah admits to Shaw, "...Now I realize it's my fault that he [killed the mole]," elaborating, "...He said he wouldn't even be here if it wasn't for me, and he's right." The other interpretative option is complete self-delusion. So who's really changing?

Sarah's crisis expands beyond the emotional and existential spheres to ultimately invade the moral realm as well, given her double standards. From "vs. the Pink Slip" forward, Sarah despises and punishes Chuck for pursuing the very goal she exhorted him to pursue during the first two seasons. It was Sarah who asked Chuck, "How many times do you have to be a hero before you realize that you are that man?" Chuck also links his decision in Prague to following the model she set, claiming, "...You're the one who taught me that being a spy is...about putting aside your own personal feelings for the greater good, and that's what I chose... to help people..." (vs. the Three Words). Moreover, her encouragement continues in the current arc during the mission impersonating Rafe the assassin. When Chuck confesses his fear while Sarah pseudo-arrests him as a SWAT agent to maintain his cover, she privately coaches him to "live the lie!" (vs. the Fake Name). And when he does just that, saving Casey's life in the process, she sees it as an impediment to their relationship despite the greater good achieved.

Additional double standards revolve around the next epic echo of Season 3: the Red Test, whose terminology notably has no basis in the actual espionage world. Just as the Red Sea posed a formidable barrier to escaping Egypt and reaching the Promised Land, the Red Test threatens to keep Chuck and Sarah separated when she creates a dubious litmus test for Chuck that creates a no-win scenario for him. On the one hand, she equates completing the Red Test by killing the rogue spy as confirmation that Chuck has fundamentally changed, thereby making him "not the same guy that I fell for" (vs. the American Hero). On the other hand, when Chuck asks whether there is any way they can be together if he does not pass his spy test, Sarah's reply is "probably not" (vs. the Final

Examination). If she is not still willing to run with him, as at the beginning of the season, what other options does that leave Chuck?

This standard makes even less sense when one considers that Sarah, as well as her current lover Shaw, kills to protect others and herself with relative regularity without seeing it as a fundamental flaw that prevents her from loving Chuck. That's to say nothing of her border-line execution of Mauser in Season 2 (vs. the Santa Claus). Additionally, Sarah initially and emphatically refuses to be a party to the test. "I can't," she tells Shaw. "Can't be a part of it. And I won't. You have to meet him. I can't make him do something like that. I'm not even sure that I want him to be able to do something like that" (vs. the Final Examination). Then she does an about-face and dispassionately meets Chuck to give him his kill order under the guise of providing Chuck with the resolve to defend himself against a "seasoned agent" like Hunter Perry, "who will do anything to save himself." So Sarah really is concerned that "we may lose [Chuck]" after all? But not enough to be with him. Sarah doesn't maintain her standard when killing affects her own well-being either. After Chuck later saves her life in Paris by 'killing' Shaw, Sarah responds with gratitude and even passion, but when Chuck supposedly shoots the mole after taking every measure to avoid doing so simply to save his own life, he disqualifies himself from her affection. This irrational version of Sarah is one viewers don't recognize.

Despite the growing distance between Chuck and Sarah as she continues to wander, Episodes 10-12 each still present moments in which Sarah does not seem entirely beyond rediscovering the path back to Chuck. In "vs. the Tic Tac," with Shaw out of town and Sarah planning to meet up with him for a "personal" weekend, Sarah ironically shifts a conversation about Casey's apparent change to Chuck, confessing, "I thought you had changed." Chuck initially keeps his feelings to himself, figured by silently stowing his ammo in his bag, zipping it shut, and pulling the harness on his back before snapping the buckle shut. Meanwhile, Sarah pleads, "…Please don't lose that guy I met three years ago. Don't give up on the things that make you great." Chuck, refusing the pistol she pushes toward him, replies, "I'll always be that guy." After the long pause that ensues, Chuck finally attempts to engage her, but Sarah, likely sensing the impending collapse of her defenses, suddenly changes the topic.

In Episode 11 (vs. the Final Exam), Chuck's charm reduces Sarah from an objective proctor of his spy certification to a glassy-eyed romantic within minutes. Moved by his nostalgic champagne, sizzling shrimp, and "Private Eyes" soundtrack, a suddenly somber Sarah can't help but softly agree with Chuck when he only half-jokingly asserts, "You're going to miss me in D.C., you know that, right?" Sarah becomes preoccupied with the refocusing of her feelings, implied by the binoculars glued to her eyes. This image mirrors Chuck's prior clarification of his feelings about Sarah when using the site of the sniper rifle to observe the scene in Shaw's hotel room. By the time Chuck pointedly asks whether she's "willing to give it another shot" if he passes his spy test, she silently answers by removing the glasses and leaning towards him in anticipation of a kiss interrupted by Shaw's radioed rebuke. And when she returns to Castle, Sarah proceeds to cover for their missing the rogue agent's entry into the hotel without so much as even looking at Shaw.

However, this promise of reconciliation lasts only as long as it takes for Chuck to supposedly kill the mole in his Red Test. And though Chuck, just returned from D.C., earnestly pleads with her in Castle to believe that something happened other than what she thinks she saw, she replies, "I don't!" But even as Shaw ushers Chuck away for some advice on Rome, Sarah's blank stare prior to her eyes following his exit suggest his words have her thinking.

When Chuck crashes her dinner date with Shaw the night before she leaves for D.C., the crux of the matter remains: who killed the mole if he did not? After pleading for one last secret before a life of no secrets, Chuck inverts Sarah's central claim: "Listen, I know you think I'm not that same guy you met the first day at the Buy More, and... you're right... The guy that I was back then hated himself for not knowing what he wanted to do for the rest of his life or who he wanted to spend it with, but now...I know. I want to be a spy. And I want to be with you." Softening once again, Sarah, with an open expression, inquires, "What are you saying?" But Shaw and Awesome crash through the window before Chuck can reply.

Just when the viewer thinks no more nooks or crannies remain in which to get lost, another appears. When a hopeful Chuck comes looking for Sarah in Castle the next day, he is treated instead to Sarah's responsive farewell kiss with the suicide mission-bent Shaw. Citing her care for Shaw, Chuck locks Sarah down and risks his life to save him. Chuck becomes, again, a hero for saving the American hero and given full credit by Sarah to Beckman, who signs off her Castle briefing with wishes for

Sarah's "safe flight." Even though Sarah, conflicted, makes no mention of a change in plans to meet Beckman in D. C., the moment she muses over her "highly memorable three years in Burbank," her face, hidden from the silently arriving Chuck behind her, immediately betrays strained, watery eyes over a crooked frown. But the moment Chuck announces his presence, she flashes a magically composed smile when she whirls around to thank him.

Thus begins Chuck's "blunt" 11th hour appeal to Sarah, highlighted by his repeated, forthright admission of love for her. Still resistant, Sarah notes commitments she has made, "and not just to Shaw." But this time Chuck, no longer confused or intimidated by her emotional walls, rams right through them, persisting in relaying his vision for a real future together. When Chuck proves willing to run away with her, now that he is a certified spy, it further conveys that he chooses Sarah over the spy life he cherishes, reversing his decision in Prague. Still conflicted, Sarah allows Chuck's kiss, the second she has received in Castle the very same day from two men, and though she does not respond demonstratively, she appears a bit woozy when parting.

Even if the dialogue in Sarah's hotel room is ambiguous, the audio-visual elements of the scene that follows argue for Sarah's decision to change course and run with Chuck even before Shaw reveals his dark baptism or Casey reveals that he shot the mole. The clock reads 6:10 PM while Sarah packs, and the short drive from downtown will easily allow her to make the 7:00 PM rendezvous at (re-)Union Station, even after she, significantly, showers and changes her clothes. Next to the clock stands the photo of Chuck and Sarah pointedly missing on her side table in the last hotel room scene, when Sarah confessed she no longer loved Chuck to Shaw after his Red Test. Would she resurrect it to grace her packing only to leave for D.C. and a life with another man? Clearly she's thinking about Chuck. The reappearance of the photo also meshes with the lyrics of "Down River," by Temper Tramp that accents both Chuck's 11th hour appeal to Sarah in Castle and the aftermath of Casey telling Sarah that he shot the mole, thematically linking the scenes:

> Finally we have seen some things
> Some awfully nice
> Some dreadfully bad
> But we will sing

Wash the blood off our knees
'Cause our love breaks through rough seas our ship will sail
And I don't understand how this world would work
'Cause time will tell us nothing
I'll take a chance on something
Feeling old, feelings this time take you
Down river, down river, down river, down
Walk these stairs, put the pieces back together
Go don't stop, go don't stop, go don't stop now, go

Regardless, Casey's confession to shooting the mole and Sarah's response leaves no doubt as to her destination when she tosses her pistol on the bed before heading to the door.

Thus, Chuck and Sarah at long last succeed in passing through the deep waters of the Red Test and exit their wilderness wandering. Except Chuck doesn't know it yet. When Shaw shows up to "settle an old score," Sarah is unable to contact Chuck before leaving. From there the attention focuses on Chuck's reprimand from Beckman for excessive force in his attempted and presumed unnecessary rescue of Sarah, though she sincerely thanks him for it before good-naturedly tweaking him about the tank. Once again unable to decipher The Blonde, Chuck sinks into a "drunken haze" thinking she's still D.C.-bound when she comes over for the famous scene affirming her love for him, though the Three Words never actually cross her lips.

But Chuck and Sarah do not actually reach the border of their Promised Land until standing on a bridge crossing a river, not the Jordan but the Seine. Indeed, it is only after Chuck shoots the treacherous Shaw in Paris—perhaps his authentic Red Test/Red Sea crossing, given the vividly crimson overcoat Sarah wears throughout the scene--that Chuck and Sarah are finally free to cross and enter in. Thus, the nondescript Nerd Herder, pointedly chosen by Bryce Larkin to receive the Intersect while he was quietly shepherding a flock of Buy Morons, moves forward with his future and not-so-coincidentally-named wife, Sarah, to settle a land of promise. But plenty of Philistines lie in wait.

CHAPTER 13:

Operation Isis

The camera hovers high above the bed. Looming below, a younger Mary Elizabeth Bartowski, aka CIA Agent Frost, reads a bedtime story to her "little Chuck" in a flashback to his childhood. The two initially hang inverted within the frame, which slowly begins to spiral as the words of the story continue: "And the king was free, and the castle was restored, and the Frost Queen returned home once more. This time she was a hero. And the Frost Queen promised her children that she would never, ever leave ever them again." By the time Mary finishes the last sentence of the story, mother and child appear upright within the frame, and she kisses her son before moving towards the door. But 9-year-old Chuck stops her. "Mom, are you going away again?" "Just for a few days," she replies, "and right back to you and Ellie." And when Chuck tells her, "I love you," she turns to assure him, "Not nearly as much as I love you." Things didn't quite work out as planned: she disappeared for roughly fifteen years.

This combination of word and image, the opening sequence of Season 4, implies that the mystery surrounding Mary Bartowski will unwind itself over the course of the season while also hinting that the issues within her family and the CIA stemming from her extended absence will be largely righted by its conclusion. The saga of Agent Frost's unorthodox return to her family does in fact dominate the season. But while the Frost Queen fairy tale notably parallels the forthcoming plotline, another figure more fully unwinds the textured mystery of Mary Bartowski: the code name for the CIA mission that severed her from her nine-year-old son and his older sister, Project Isis.

Ancient Egyptian mythology invested Isis, a major goddess, with several definitive traits. Among the most prominent, Isis served as a personification of the Pharaoh's throne and as such a representation of his power. Indeed, her headdress, commonly fashioned in the shape of a throne, highlighted this function. Not coincidentally, the picture on the cover of the fairy tale from which Frost reads shows the Frost Queen sitting on an icy throne.

Agent Frost, in the deep cover Project Isis, rises to a similar position of authority within her target: global arms dealer Volkoff Industries, viciously run from Moscow by Alexei Volkoff. Although Chuck and his partners do not meet his mother until Episode 6 (vs. the Aisle of Terror), they become aware of her involvement in an underground arms pipeline called Operation Beacon early in the season, and Chuck naturally homes in on this signal to extract any information available regarding his mother. The early testimony suggests that Agent Frost has worked her way up to a high level within the Volkoff organization. In "vs. the Cubic Z," Heather Chandler finally spills the fact that during her dealing with Volkoff, Frost "was always around" him, and in the next episode (vs. the Coup D'état), the Costa Gravan premier, who purchased Russian nuclear arms using Operation Beacon, confirms Frost's intimate association with Volkoff as "some kind of a kept woman."

These early clues of having penetrated the select inner circle are definitively confirmed by none other than Volkoff himself, who later calls her "my right hand" (vs. the Gobbler). Indeed, she demonstrates the unique privilege of walking boldly into Volkoff's office unbidden, registering her protest over his accepting Sarah's rogue services, and providing frank, unsolicited advice that Sarah will betray him. And when Frost concocts the idea of sending Sarah on a "suicide mission" to break out Uri the Gobbler as a test, Volkoff immediately approves it. Of course, the reason for her elevated position within Volkoff's hierarchy stems from his bizarre affection for her, an affection Frost forcefully manipulates on occasion. In the Echo Park courtyard after the Thanksgiving leftovers dinner party, she makes it brutally clear, with a gun pointed at Volkoff's head, "I will not return with you until you promise me that my family and their friends will remain safe. And if they don't, I will end you." The master of fear himself pays her the ultimate compliment when speaking to her son, who needs a lesson in that department, even while backing down: "You see, that is a real threat" (vs. the Leftovers).

Aside from the authoritative symbolism associated with Isis, ancient Egyptians deemed her a patroness of deception, even magic. And if nothing else, Agent Frost keeps everyone guessing as to exactly who she is and what side she is on as she attempts to walk the thin tightrope between her family, the CIA, and Volkoff. Chuck certainly displays issues with trusting her ironic actions, though she attempts to provide him with clues. At the meet Frost sets up between Chuck, posing as Charles Carmichael, and Dr. Wheelright selling the Atroxium (vs. the Aisle of Terror), she shows up unexpectedly, even though the transaction appears to be progressing well. After pointedly stating, for Chuck's benefit, "Sometimes appearances don't tell the whole story," she proceeds to announce she has done some digging on Carmichael and declares him a spy. Within seconds, she pulls a gun, shoots Chuck in the chest, eliminates the surveillance camera feed, and disappears with the scientist and nerve gas. And when Frost subsequently drops by the Buy More to pick up Chuck for an impromptu joy ride, she forgets she keeps him at gunpoint until Chuck points out the dicey nature of the situation. "I'm sorry," she says while laying the pistol down, "I have to keep up appearances." And after dropping Chuck off at the mobile lab at the docks, Chuck sees her as a magician reversing the rabbit trick: "You're gonna vanish for good now, aren't you?" This is to say nothing of her later, apparent attempt to blow Chuck up along with the old family homestead.

Chuck's Castle partners are fooled into thinking Frost rogue, too. Casey obtains expunged files on Operation Isis, concluding it "ended 20 years ago when Frost went rogue." After telling Sarah that everything is fake and that Frost is a double agent, he regrets not nabbing her before she vanished. Sarah, fessing up that Frost is meeting Ellie prior to disappearing, signs on to the abduction of Frost, telling Chuck that she's watching "his blind spot" after the fact. However, when Sarah later reverses course and places her faith in Frost, at Chuck's request, Frost ends up duping both of them again when she tricks them into revealing the secret base, suppressing the Intersect in Chuck's brain, and allowing Volkoff to blow up the base (vs. the First Fight). In that scene, Volkoff lauds Frost as nothing less than "a master of deception." Alas, he, too, finds himself a victim. When her betrayal of him is in the open at last on the Countessa, Volkoff, pushed to the edge of his sanity, pines, "I believed in you."

As highlighted in the season's opening sequence, a higher purpose looms beyond Frost's deceptions: the safety of her beloved family. Not surprisingly, Isis was worshiped as a motherly goddess of children and particularly protective of her own son, Horus. In an intriguing extension, some scholars link the iconography of the Madonna and Child to the influence of similar imagery connected to the Isis cult that preceded it. Though Mary's abandonment of her family, like Orion's, wreaks of moral failure on the surface, it was her care for them, ironically, that caused her to leave, remain hidden, and want to know nothing about them when she thinks it necessary to return, at least initially.

In "vs. the Anniversary," viewers see the decidedly frosty side of this motherly love. When informed by a Volkoff underling and his henchmen in Moscow that her family is looking for her, Frost asks if they have informed Volkoff of this news. When assured they have not, a visibly relieved Frost Queen replies, "That is good…That is very, very good," prior to ambushing them and leaving behind a trail of riddled corpses. Before she pulls the final trigger, the underling pleads, "I have a family." Frost's icy reply? "So do I."

When Frost does finally meet Chuck face to face for the first time in fifteen years (vs. the Aisle of Terror), she tells her wide-eyed son, "I don't want to know anything about you. I am deep under cover in the Volkoff organization. And if they do blow my cover, they will torture me for secrets. I don't want to know one thing about you or your sister that could put you in danger." Subsequently, she helps him to see that her shooting him ("I knew you had a vest on"), suppressing the Intersect ("It was to stop [you] from following me"), and appearing to blow up Chuck and the base were acts of care from her perspective, as they would keep him out of the reach of her utterly ruthless target, Alexei Volkoff. She then moonlights by 'supervising' the assassin team sent to eliminate Chuck to ensure that they fail (vs. the Leftovers).

When Chuck tries to grasp her altruistic motives, stating, "You did this to protect me and Ellie?" Frost makes a transparent confession: "Chuck, you and your sister are and always have been my only concern. Not being in your lives has pained me more than you could ever imagine…I constantly relive that day when I walked out the door. Over and over. And I want you to know that if I could do it over again, I never would have left. I would still be there with my family" (vs. the Aisle of Terror). And in her moment of utmost vulnerability, with Chuck's death apparently imminent at the hands of Volkoff in the Buy More, Frost reveals Chuck's identity as her son to Volkoff, adding, "I'm sorry, Alexei. My one weakness is my love for my son…" (vs. the Leftovers). Similarly, when Volkoff's gun is trained on Sarah after the leftovers meal, Frost risks pointing her muzzle at Alexei's head, explaining, "This is exactly why I didn't tell you about my family." Upon leaving, she apologizes to Chuck, admitting, "I hope that someday you'll trust me." A convert, Chuck's response is immediate: "Mom, I already do." As Sarah clearly understands the next morning, "She's the only thing that's keeping us safe."

Though Sarah is not technically Frost's child, her significant linkage to Chuck and, notably, Sarah's utmost desire to protect Chuck draws Frost increasingly toward Sarah like a daughter, too. During an interrogation in "vs. the First Fight," Sarah informs Frost, "I can't protect your son if I don't know where he is." Frost later pointedly observes Chuck holding Sarah's hand in the elevator while on the way to meet Volkoff in the Buy More (vs. the Leftovers) and Sarah running to his side to cradle him when struck by Volkoff minutes later. Knowing also that Sarah's abduction of her was motivated by a desire to protect her son, Frost passes the baton to Sarah when she must, again, disappear into the shadow world after blowing up Orion's secret base. Leaving her bound future daughter-in-law with the razor blade, not Chuck, she whispers, "Protect him."

This bond strengthens and even expands into a mentor role in "vs. The Gobbler" and "vs. the Push Mix," when Sarah takes the ultimate risk of joining Volkoff in order to bring Chuck's mother home. At the first opportune moment, Frost secretly meets with Sarah, who has just ingratiated herself to Volkoff by leaving him unharmed at gunpoint, to prepare her for what may come: "Sarah, I need you to realize that going undercover in a place like this can require certain difficult choices…You may find yourself becoming something you no longer recognize." After throwing Casey out a high-rise window, these words take on new meaning. And on the plane ride home from that horrific assignment, uncertain if Casey is permanently maimed, Mary reaches out to Sarah across the seat and takes her hand. "It gets easier." "How?" Sarah whispers. "Distance." Sarah proceeds to decline Chuck's call. Ultimately, Frost lovingly insists that Sarah terminate her self-assignment to Volkoff and return to Chuck. While on the cusp of the Countessa mission, Frost orders, "Tonight, whether or not we find the Hydra, you're going home…. I don't want you to become me. And I will not allow my son to become his father. So, tonight, it ends." Sarah offers no argument.

As with many mother-in-laws, Sarah and Frost still deal with their occasional issues. On the eve of her wedding, Sarah ends up guarding the cell door of Frost, who insists she does not need to be rescued, claiming, "Chuck knows that I can take care of myself." Sarah disagrees, citing her failure to arrange back-up, two days before their wedding, no less. As it turns out, it is a good thing Sarah was there after all when Vivian Volkoff and her key aide Reilly show up to execute the woman who betrayed her father. Later, while Chuck appreciates his mom trying to protect them by assuming control of their own mission and offering to travel back to Moscow alone with Morgan, he stands up to her. Even as Frost insists that she is stepping in to "fix your mistake," Sarah insists they will be going on the mission, and Mary will serve as back-up.

Thankfully, Frost shows some self-awareness after accepting her reserve role. While on the mission, she chooses to give Chuck and Sarah, in the van, a little space, but on the rooftop she laments to Casey, "It's hard to have kids. Can't always protect them." Casey sympathizes, "Or their idiot boyfriends." And Frost is right. When Chuck's life is almost taken by Reilly, Sarah saves him before Frost can arrive and get off the shot that would have been too late. Recognizing a woman after her own heart, Frost makes public her personal affection for Sarah in a toast at the reception:

> Now that I'm back in [Chuck's and Sarah's] lives, I sometimes overcompensate. But lucky for me, my soon-to-be daughter-in-law is very forgiving. She's never heard me say it, but Sarah is one of the strongest and one of the most amazing women that I have ever met. So I would like to propose this toast to her. Sarah, thank you for taking care of my Chuck. May you have many more adventures together, and may you always keep each other safe.

And speaking of overcompensation, Frost does the same with her granddaughter, Baby Clara. Enchanted with the fragile infant at her birth, Frost proceeds to integrate herself into Ellie and Awesome's life to help them with the transition (for more on Mary's relationship with Ellie, see Chapter 17: Missing Links). But in the end, too much. Wanting to fill the lack created by her prolonged separation from her children, Mary confesses, "I want to give everything to this baby that I never gave to you and Chuck" (vs. the Seduction Impossible). Softly, Ellie reminds her mother, "That's my job. You just have to be the best grandma in the world," before giving a blessing for her return to spy work. And only occasionally does Frost violate the rule of no guns in sight of the baby.

In a final link between Frost and Isis, both serve in the role of grieving widow. Though Frost does not weep enough tears to fill the Nile, as Isis did after the death of King Osiris, she does declare her admiration and devotion for Orion. With her cover finally blown and facing likely execution on the Countessa, Frost remains behind to allow the rest of the Castle team to escape. Having just received the pseudo-Orion message, Volkoff accuses Frost of knowing Orion was alive through the years and cites it as the reason Frost has kept herself apart from him. With nothing to lose, Frost finally unbinds her tightly wound feelings: "The truth is, my husband, alive or dead, will always be ten times the man you are. And every moment that I was with you, I was thinking of him."

The expression of her devotion has the uncanny effect of making Volkoff vow to bring Frost back Orion's corpse before pressing his own lips against hers in a kiss she wipes away. However, there is another kiss that Mary will never wipe from her memory. When Ellie asks her to elaborate on the story told to Clara and identify the man who "kissed you awake on your secret mission," Mary clearly relishes informing her of the "big romantic. And the greatest husband there ever was" (vs. the Seduction Impossible).

CHAPTER 14:

Phase Three

The title of Season 4's Episode 9, "Chuck vs. Phase Three," literally alludes to the third and final stage of Dr. Mueller's nefarious probe into the mind of Chuck. In order to isolate and activate the Intersect, Phase Three calls for erasing all other elements of Chuck's mind, potentially "lobotomizing" him and leaving him a vegetable. On a metaphorical level, however, the title calls attention to the third stage of Chuck and Sarah's relationship. After cover dating, followed by a period of real, exclusive dating, they linger on the cusp of entering the final phase: engagement and marriage. Viewed within this framework, the events presented in both "vs. the Fear of Death" and "vs. Phase Three" provide insights into both Chuck's and Sarah's deepest insecurities as they grapple with issues pertaining to their future together.

When Mary Bartowski suppresses the Intersect in an ironic attempt to protect Chuck (vs. the First Fight), it upends Chuck's personal world as well as his professional one. In Chuck's mind, the development not only threatens his identity as a spy but, consequently, the status of his relationship with Sarah. Chuck, who usually wears his heart on his sleeve, keeps his fear regarding the latter hidden even as it increasingly causes him to jeopardize, unbeknownst to him, that which he already possesses: a future with a committed partner who loves him uncondition-ally. Meanwhile, Chuck's actions launch the usually guarded Sarah to unprecedented levels of desperation and vulnerability that reveal her own fundamental need for Chuck.

Chuck doesn't hide the fact that the Intersect's suppression, leaving him unable to flash, also leaves him anxious about his future as a spy. The prospects of working simply as an analyst, assuming an offer from Beckman, or even worse at the Buy More prove unappealing.

Beyond that, it puts the future of Project Bartowski at risk. As Casey tells Alex over lunch, he will likely be sent to Afghanistan or Iraq with no Intersect to drive the Burbank operation, and Sarah will also likely face reassignment. When Sarah, returned from abroad, asks Chuck if the myriad of tests conducted to retrieve/activate the Intersect have yielded any results, Chuck candidly jokes, "You would have heard my giant sigh of relief, even in Moscow." Concerned over the toll the process is taking on Chuck, Sarah pleads, "Promise me you're not doing it for me or us." Speaking only half of the truth, Chuck replies, "No, no. I'm doing it for the team. I've never been a spy without the Intersect. And I quite like being a spy. Doing great things. Doing them with you. I want that back." Pressure from the rest of the Castle crew doesn't help. Casey increasingly suffers from an "itchy trigger finger," a condition driving his Buy More manager to distraction, and both proceed to voice their concerns to Chuck, who confesses, "Nobody wants to put the team back together more than me; you've got to know that." Sarah, compelled to step in, assures them, "He gets it."

While open about his concern over continuing his career as a spy, Chuck masks a deeper fear: losing his future with Sarah due to the loss of the Intersect. This is not primarily the fault of Sarah, who voices her desire to marry a supposedly sleeping Chuck a few episodes prior when Chuck still retains the Intersect (vs. the Coup D'état). Indeed, she provides general encouragement in the midst of Chuck's present difficulties. While giving him a rub down in the bedroom, she assures him, "You don't need the Intersect to do great things. You're great on your own." When Chuck counters, "But am I a spy?" Sarah hesitates briefly, before replying, "Yes.. Yes, but you're Chuck Bartowski, and you do that all on your own." To validate her heart-warming words, she leans down to leave a kiss on his cheek before retrieving the warming oil. Later, as Chuck is about to depart for Gstaadt, she will plead with Chuck, "Don't be a hero. Just come home safe to me."

Uncharacteristically, the usually garrulous Chuck never consciously verbalizes his fear of losing Sarah, but the text communicates it in a variety of indirect ways nonetheless. Morgan's comments to Sarah while she languishes in the bedroom after Chuck is taken captive indicate that he and Chuck have discussed a similar issue. After Sarah inquires about the engagement proposal plan she finds in Chuck's shirt pocket, Morgan informs her, "…Ever since he lost the Intersect, the proposal plan got put on hold." When Sarah betrays confusion, Morgan elaborates, "It's just that…you're kind of a big fish, you know, and to a regular guy with no supercomputer in his brain…I think that that's pretty intimidating." Unsettled by Morgan's revelation, Sarah asks, "Did he think that I wouldn't want to marry him without the Intersect? Is that how I made him feel?" As she begins to connect the dots, Sarah stands up to clarify, "That's not the reason I love Chuck. I do want to spend my life with Chuck, with or without the Intersect!" Rising to his own feet, Morgan expresses visible relief: "Fantastic! That's great! Yeah, and he knows that, right? Because you told him that." Sarah's anguished expression suffices as her reply of silent regret.

Morgan's explicit indication of Chuck's anxiety over losing Sarah is supported by additional if more subtle clues. Elements of the dream sequences, induced by Dr. Mueller to probe into Chuck's sub consciousness and unlock the Intersect, prove noteworthy in this regard. Dr. Mueller introduces thoughts of abandonment into the "neurotic man's" mind in his attempt to scare Chuck into flashing, and while Mueller is indeed responsible for inserting the thoughts into his mind, Chuck's responses to them provide a window to his perhaps repressed fear.

In the first dream sequence, rather than reject thoughts of abandonment, Chuck's mind envisions a disdainful Sarah dismounting Chuck and sulking, no longer interested in him when he cannot heed her appeals to flash. In a subsequent sequence, Sarah rolls her suitcase towards the apartment door while Chuck pleads, "Sarah, please don't go. I can't lose you. I'll do anything!" Accordingly, Mueller informs The Belgian, "This woman will do most of the work. No one makes him more anxious than this..Sarah Walker." But Lester has an intriguing cameo as well. In the first dream sequence, lying on the other side of Chuck from Sarah, he notably does not also appeal for Chuck to flash, as one would expect given Sarah's response; instead Lester keeps the focus on Sarah, asking, "…You really expect to keep a girl like that without flashing?" followed by a diabolical laugh.

This dynamic is reinforced by the pointed imagery developing these episodes. Agent Rye figures the culprit weighing down the Intersect as a "psychological rock," recalling the 'rock' on an engagement ring and, thus, the proposal Chuck is putting on hold until the Intersect is reactivated. This view gains more credence when one remembers the mission on which Chuck embarks to reactivate the Intersect and supposedly preserve his future with Sarah not only features stealing a 100-carat rock but specifically a diamond. Moreover, Rye ultimately identifies Sarah as the "emotional rock" sitting on the Intersect. Chuck asks Rye why his therapy isn't working since he truly feared for his life in the diamond vault, and Rye replies, "The psychological rock is keyed on to a..deeper anxiety..person..a relationship." And when Chuck inquires which relationship that is, Rye pulls out Chuck's cell phone with Sarah's picture before answering, "With her." It is no coincidence either that Rye implicitly links the reactivation of the Intersect with the temporary status of Chuck's romantic relationship by asking the ultimate question: "…Are you a spy, or a guy with a spy girlfriend?"

In a separate figure, Agent Rye personifies Chuck's unspoken fear of losing Sarah in a striking reprise of the scene involving a masked Carina to figure Sarah's hidden fear in Season 1 (see Chapter 2: Fish Out of Water). Just after Chuck and Sarah pointedly discuss his motivation for submitting to the tortuous experiments of Agent Rye, a conversation in which Chuck denies he is doing it for Sarah or them, Rye silently sneaks into their bedroom fully masked as a pseudo ninja warrior to thrust a pair of swords over his neck. The scare tactic fails in activating the Intersect, but the comments that follow about the intrusiveness of the unwelcome prowler are intriguing. Chuck shouts, "Honey, we have company!" And when Sarah rushes in with a knife, she demands to know, "What are you doing in our home!?" Chuck's deep-seated fear has entered into the most private recesses of their relationship, and three is a dangerous crowd.

In the first dream sequence, Lester states to Chuck, "This is all in your head. You have got to get over this." Ignorant of this fact, a desperate Chuck will "do anything" to not simply maintain an espionage career but, perhaps subconsciously, also appease his insecurity over Sarah. When the extreme measures to resurrect the Intersect in secured situations with Agent Rye fail to produce a result, Rye recommends similar situations in unsecured situations to achieve the extreme fear necessary. "Castle's a safety zone," Rye explains, "and apparently [your home] is, too." The Gstaadt mission "fits the bill" as "incredibly…dangerous" with a "guaranteed…threat of violence." Though Sarah calls the mission "crazy," Chuck is committed to "whatever it takes to get the Intersect back." Sarah attempts to have Beckman assign Casey and her to the mission as back-up, but Rye argues against it, citing the need for total fear. When Chuck explains that there needs to be no safety net for him to flash, Sarah counters, "Yes, Chuck, but then there's no safety net!"

The mission enters its second and more dangerous stage after Chuck and Rye discover the microdots contained in the fake diamonds. During a video conference broadcast to Sarah and Casey in Castle, Beckman acknowledges, "This is Code Red and could likely get very ugly." Sarah immediately requests permission to travel to Gstaadt to serve as back-up. Thus begins an exchange that crystallizes the increased tension in Chuck's and Sarah's respective dilemmas:

> **Chuck:** Um, I think Sarah should let us handle this, seeing as how we have determined this is the only way I will get the Intersect back working.
>
> **Sarah:** Chuck, we're talking about real danger now.
>
> **Chuck:** I'm sorry, and I can only handle fake danger?
>
> **Sarah:** Look, I know the Intersect is important, but so far none of Agent Rye's therapies have worked. And the microdot contains highly sensitive information that the wrong people will.kill.for.
>
> **Chuck:** Well, I can take care of these wrong people without you holding my hand.
>
> **Sarah:** Why does it make sense to risk your life?!
>
> **Chuck:** Because it's what I do: I am a spy.
>
> **Sarah:** No, Chuck! You're not!....Not right now.

Ironically, Sarah's attempt to preserve Chuck goads him into taking the supreme risk. Given the option to wait for Sarah or arrest the Belgian and "be heroes," Chuck replies, "Let's be heroes." As they step on to the gondola, an "enclosed space [with] no escape," to confront the Belgian and his henchmen, Rye says, "Last chance, Chuck. On or off?" Chuck makes his choice: "On." But his failure to flash soon leaves him dangling from the edge. With his fingers slipping, Chuck comes to the tardy epiphany that "I would rather love Sarah than have the Intersect," but after Rye is killed and his corpse plunges to earth, Chuck finds himself at the mercy of his adversary. And there is no mercy.

Chuck's desperate attempt to retain his identity as a spy and preserve his future with Sarah ironically ignites her own identity crisis and emotional free fall, imaged by her fragmented face, half-hidden in the bedding, after she falls distraught on the bed. There are a few causes for this psychological plunge. In one regard, it does not take long for Sarah to recognize she is not the same person without Chuck. Out of character, Sarah challenges General Beckman during briefings after Chuck's capture, impatient with the progress of the manhunt. Beckman denies Sarah authorization to leave for Belgium and "hunt down the son-of-a-bitch" before telling her to go home. Sarah, barely able to contain her pacing, jabs her finger to the table and defiantly vows, "I'm staying right here," leading to an order for her to leave Castle. In the next conference, Sarah treats Beckman, who assures her the government has a vested interest in keeping Chuck's secrets, with even more insolence, shouting, "Forget the secrets! This is about Chuck!"

And it gets worse. Upon 'welcoming' Thai diplomat Anand Chanarong to American soil after his kidnapping, Sarah digresses into a former version of herself. Morgan, worried Sarah is going to go "Kill Bill" after observing her interrogate the Thai national, notifies Casey, who confirms Morgan's observation and tells her, "You need to cool down...You're acting like a spy I used to know, before Chuck: Langston Graham's wild card enforcer. I didn't like that Sarah Walker...because she was unpredictable." It takes Morgan wedging himself between the two to avoid a physical confrontation. After later kicking Casey into a detention cell, allowing her free reign to 'interrogate' Chanarong with the threat of an illegal ammonia injection, Sarah reappears to tell Casey, "You were right. I'm different without Chuck, and I don't like it." Moments later, she stomps out of Castle bound for Thailand alone, but not before confessing to Casey, "I need Chuck." This claim recalls her words to Dr. Dreyfuss in "vs. the Tooth" when, as Chuck's sanity appears to be slipping away, Sarah confides, "I need him to be OK." In this context, Sarah's half-submerged face in the swamp at The Belgian's compound serves as a baptismal image of her changed self without Chuck, while, along with her black attire, also reprising a darkened Col. Kurtz in another Southeast Asian jungle swamp in "Apocalypse Now."

In addition to unraveling Sarah's evolving sense of self, Chuck's capture threatens the dream of the future with Chuck Sarah has secretly nursed since Season 1 (see Chapter 2: Fish Out of Water and Chapter 4: A Slow and Painful Awakening). As early as the end of Season 2, Sarah determines to choose Chuck over the spy life if necessary (see Chapter 10: Tug of War), though he remains unaware of it. Similarly, Sarah informs Casey she's not going to leave the CIA headquarters and run in the Season 3 finale because, with Chuck in custody, "everything I care about is in this building." It is clear, however, that Sarah has thought specifically about marriage and even family, too.

Earlier in Season 4, Sarah informs a supposedly sleeping Chuck that she would say yes to a proposal, and when Morgan claims Chuck was planning to propose, she greets the news with eagerness. By the time Sarah, syringe in hand, informs Chanarong that the man she's looking for "loves me; he wants to marry me," her enthusiasm borders on the maniacal. But their conversation expands to include the topic of children as well when the Thai mocks, "Even the toughest spies in the world are just racing against that biological clock. Tick, tick, tick..tock." Sarah doesn't make the slightest effort to defend herself or deny his claim. On the contrary, she freely concedes his point, seemingly without irony: "You got me!...I'm just a needy, love-crazed girl on a husband hunt...." This unprecedented transparency will be matched in the series only when she is finally reunited with Chuck in The Belgian's compound.

A final cause of Sarah's emotional free fall is that she holds herself responsible for Chuck's risk-taking and even betrays traces of self-loathing. Soon after Chuck is taken captive, she laments to Casey, daggers in her eyes, "This is all my fault. He did this to prove to me that he could be a spy," before storming out of Castle. And this is before her subdued exchange with Morgan, in which, after hearing Chuck put the proposal plan on hold, she asks, "Why? Did he think that I wouldn't want to marry him without the Intersect? Is that the way I made him feel?" The scene leaves her in anguished silence. Thus, when Sarah informs the Thai that the ammonia will kill him by burning him from the inside out, she implies her own emotional hell as she rages with regret over her perceived lack of communication.

"I'll do anything to get him back:" Sarah, whose desperate words mirror those Chuck speaks in one dream sequence, means what she says. Just as she was willing to pull the trigger to preserve her dream of a future with Chuck in "vs. the Santa Claus" (see Chapter 7: Thunder and Rain), Sarah is willing to risk her life and career by going rogue to find Chuck and save him from The Belgian. Her abduction of Chanarong with Casey from the sovereign soil of the Thai embassy is a violation of international law, as are her methods when interrogating him. After throwing a variety of forbidden devices on the table, she herself admits, "Normally I wouldn't threaten a subject with death by ammonia injection....Doesn't sound like something in the Geneva Convention, does it?" Sarah displays signs of instability as she proceeds with the interrogation, transforming in an instant from a love-sick girlfriend to a syringe-thrusting thug "trained in over two hundred ways to kill...." Still fully cognizant of the potential consequence of her actions, Sarah leaves for the jungles of northern Thailand without Casey, telling him, "I'm not going to bring you down with me."

Once she arrives, Sarah proceeds to create an instant legacy as the Blonde She-Male "tearing" through the jungle. After pummeling a would-be boyfriend in a sketchy bar, Sarah accepts a hand-to-hand combat to gain the location of The Belgian's compound. The victory over the champion whose only problem is that he "kills too fast" does not come without difficulty or treachery. Unfazed by the cobra roaming the pit, Sarah eventually gets the better of her opponent until he throws a handful of sand in her eyes, blinding her. However, like Sand Wall and Sandstorm before, it proves no permanent barrier to her future with Chuck. On the verge of killing Sarah with a dagger thrown from the crowd, the fighter is shocked to find the weapon blown out of his hand by the precise aim of the just-arrived Casey. And as Morgan pointedly proceeds to help her regain her sight with the help of some water, Sarah comes to the realization that finding Chuck is not a battle she must fight alone. Pouring the balance of the canteen's contents over her head, Sarah proceeds to incapacitate her rival and turn her mascara-smeared face to demand, "Now where's Chuck?!"

Chuck's and Sarah's struggles converge in The Belgian's laboratory. As Dr. Mueller initiates Phase Three, Chuck suffers a series of earthquakes that signal the impending disintegration of his mind, even as his future with Sarah approaches erasure. The Belgian leans over a non-responsive Chuck to ask, "What do you think it feels like to watch your life disappear?" The answer emerges as lights begin to shut off and friends communicate artificially via plasma screen, mercilessly reminding Chuck of his precarious future as a spy and with Sarah. When Ellie and Awesome appear in the flesh, the rustling breeze that accompanies them signifies Chuck's fleeting consciousness, punctuated by additional quakes. After they disappear behind a door, Chuck's shattering world is figured by glass from a broken window flying past him. As Dr. Mueller confirms to the Castle crew when it bursts in, "…He's almost completely gone."

But there is one other who still populates Chuck's imploding mind. When Sarah, sprinting to his side in the laboratory, speaks his name, the metaphorical glass immediately falls to the floor, and the disintegration pauses. Peeling off head nodes and releasing his wrist, Sarah attempts to release Chuck from his emotional bondage, assuring a skeptical Chuck she is there. Tentatively, the Nerd Herder opens a door of his mind to find her sitting in their darkened bedroom, his knight dressed all in white telling him, "I came to rescue you." From his frazzled perspective, Chuck notably perceives Sarah speaking quietly, calmly and with poise; in reality, though, the equally shattered world of a guilt-ridden Sarah, dressed in black, is on full display. Her voice breaking, her face anguished, her tears unimpeded, she pleads for the chance to fill the verbal void and douse her internal burning: "Please wake up; I have so much that I want to tell you."

Convinced Sarah is real when she describes his proposal plan, Chuck listens as Sarah reveals not only her love and desire to marry him, Intersect or not, but an epiphany that ironizes Chuck's own identity crisis: "Without you, I'm nobody. I'm nothing but a spy." After a final plea, "Come back to me, Chuck," Sarah seals her words with a Matrix-like kiss that also anticipates the "magical kiss" Sarah will ask for in an attempt to bring back her memories in the series finale. When Chuck awakes, it enables the Castle Couple to repossess an almost-forfeited Promised Land (see Chapter 12: Wandering into the Promised Land). And after Chuck later expresses relief over Beckman's offer to retain him as a spy without the Intersect, Sarah pointedly emphasizes a more significant fact: "More importantly, you're home."

"Vs. Phase Three" constitutes the emotional climax of the Castle Couple's romance. Even as Sarah rescues Chuck from both The Belgian and himself with her vows, Chuck, by heeding Sarah's appeal to return to her, likewise rescues Sarah from herself and preserves a normal life with him. From this point forward, no doubts remain over the depth and permanence of their feelings for one another, relegating their engagement and wedding to the functions of falling action and denouement, respectively.

CHAPTER 15:

Wall Comes Tumbling Down

The burly, middle-aged man crouches on all fours, his hands gripping a scrub brush, a drying towel draped over his shoulder. After scouring his roommate's taquito stain from the tiled kitchen floor, he stands up to reveal the message proudly proclaimed on his apron: World's Greatest Dad. Welcome to the world of Colonel John Casey in Season 5 (vs. Sarah), a reality he himself could not have fathomed even as late as the middle of Season 3. Especially if he happened to glimpse the identity of his roommate: Morgan Grimes. Still, when Casey turns to confront the source of the stain, the Marine formerly regarded as "the most cold-blooded sniper in the world" displays the naiveté to ask, "Do you really think I've changed?"

If living inside a wall serves as the controlling metaphor for Casey's emotional fortification in the first half of the series (see Chapter 11: The Man Who Lived in a Wall), the collapse of that wall dominates the second half. But no one said the internal demolition was going to be quick or painless. This dynamic is pointedly figured midway through Season 4 when Casey hides inside another wall, this time as part of "The Seduction Impossible" mission in Morocco involving Agent Roan Montgomery. However, this wall ultimately comes tumbling down. Narrowly escaping his own death during the machine gun execution of a dozen hoodlums on the other side, Casey finds his refuge riddled with bullet holes and his arm trapped by a portion of the fallen bearing wall, so much so that he reports to Castle he may have to cut it off to escape. Thankfully, Chuck and Sarah arrive before that is necessary and ultimately free him from the wreckage.

No catalyst proves more responsible for propelling the process of Casey's emotional liberation than the introduction of daughter Alex into his life. No sooner does he succeed in saving Kathleen, his ex-fiancé (vs. the Tic Tac) than does Casey discover he fathered a child he didn't know existed before his staged, top-secret death. This familial mission proves just as challenging but much longer, and it gets off to a slow start. Initially, Casey contents himself to incognito lunches at the Pie Shack in Silver Lake, where Alex waits on him as "Mr. Casey." But when The Ring closes in on wresting control of the CIA (vs. the Subway), Casey knows instinctively, "It's not just us they're going to come after. They're going to come after the people we care about." Though he arrives at the restaurant at the earliest opportunity, The Ring has already anticipated his move, and Casey must brutally apply the nearest napkin dispenser to the face of the rogue agent before grabbing a panicked Alex and carrying her off over his shoulder to save her life.

Clearly, this isn't the plan Casey drew up to enter into his daughter's life. And his subsequent delay in identifying himself as they sit awkwardly in the Crown Vic at a remote location doesn't endear Alex any further to her courteous abductor. But Alex's attempt to flee finally forces Casey's hand, and he reveals his identity as her father to stop her in her tracks (vs. the Ring: Part II). Initially suspicious of his claim, Alex begins to weigh its credibility more seriously when he provides details no one else would know: "You were named after your dad, Alex. You're named after me. My real name is Alex Coburn." Alex sheds her remaining skepticism shortly after arriving at the Buy More with Casey's locker key and spills her story to Manager Grimes. Without hesitation, Morgan puts the damsel at ease, saying, "Look, Miss, I promise you this: if John Casey said he's your father, then it's the truth. I trust that man with my life. You have nothing to be afraid of, not if he's your father." Willing to start anew with her father after The Ring threat is foiled, a tentative Alex shows up at the dinner party that concludes Season 3, which presents an almost speechless Casey welcoming her with an awkward hug that touches the rest of Team Bartowski.

Casey proceeds to demonstrate difficulty moving past this awkwardness, though he secretly wishes to. At first he keeps his wall up, telling Chuck that he doesn't see Alex much because "spies don't put down roots. That's the rule." Sensei Chuck gently counters, "Rule? It's not a rule. It's a notion, a suggestion or guideline." Casey becomes more honest, though, admitting to Sarah (vs. the Cubic Z), "Sometimes I think about calling. But Alex has her own life. I just don't know what my role is." Similarly, when Casey asks Morgan why he's talking to Alex (vs. the

Suitcase), Morgan confronts him with the larger issue: "More importantly, why aren't you talking to her?" Casey admits he doesn't know where he would "fit in," but Morgan counters, "You're not gonna if you don't try." The only reply Casey can muster at this point is a grunt.

Still, a crack in the wall appears by the end of the episode. In the wake of Casey's turning down an invitation to a Buy More party, Morgan again challenges Casey, asking, "How is Burbank ever going to feel like home if you never give it a chance?" Casey seems to walk away unaffected once more. That is until he pulls out his cell phone and dials a number. "Alex, hi; it's me. Dad." A smile slips across his face. "Good to hear your voice, too." Soon, Alex is bringing over soup to help the convalescence of her wounded hero (vs. the Coup D'état).

Morgan's romantic pursuit of Alex reveals more of Casey's protective side. Casey seems uncomfortable with their relationship from early on, asking questions even when they are simply sharing recipes. As matters become more serious, so do Casey's intimidating responses, so much so that Morgan at first balks at responding to Alex's advances and, later, confronting the issue with Casey. In a comic scene, a desperate Morgan finally chooses to tell Casey they are dating in order to bring him out of Couch Lock, throwing in a zinger about how Alex will soon be spending the night to achieve maximum effect. It works. Casey breaks out of his zombie-like state to hold him off the ground seized by the throat. However, just when Morgan thinks a future with Alex is over, she appears unexpectedly at his own party, suddenly impressed with him and rethinking her quitting on the relationship. Turns out she was invited by her father, who concocts the story that he changed his mind after Morgan stood up to him. However, Casey's surreptitious blessing proves no carte blanche. Even as he accepts Morgan's stammering gratitude, Casey delivers a brutal warning: "You break her heart, I break your everything."

Unfortunately for Morgan, Casey partially follows through in the aftermath of the Season 5 Morgansect arc, during which the temporarily deluded Morgan dumps Alex via text. In perhaps the largest gap in Casey's firewall evidenced in the entire series, he tries to console his heartbroken daughter, confessing, "We Caseys: we don't like to open up. Make ourselves vulnerable. 'Cuz when someone does rip our heart out and rip it open right in front of our eyes, it would be like the worst torture of all" (vs. the Frosted Tips). Even after the faulty version of the Intersect, largely responsible for bringing out Morgan's "inner jerk," is removed, Casey first asks him if he is OK...before punching him in the gut. This move is further ironic given that just a few episodes earlier Casey had saved Morgan's life in Moscow with his uncanny sniper skills (vs. the Last Details). But the deeper motive for his protection of Morgan is, again, Alex: Casey made a promise to his daughter to protect Morgan on missions, a promise he agonizes over not breaking. As Mary Bartowski laments on that mission, "Can't always protect [kids]." Casey agrees, "Yeah, or their idiot boyfriends." And when Alex is threatened by Quinn at the end of Season 5 (vs. the Bullet Train) and again later by the amnesiac Sarah (vs. Sarah), Casey leads Chuck and Sarah to Quinn and urges Chuck to give up on his quest to save Sarah, respectively, in desperate attempts to save his daughter.

Back near the end of Season 4, Casey's emerging relationship with Alex takes perhaps its most significant step forward when he is severely injured in his several-story fall at the hands of Sarah in "vs. The Gobbler." Alex stands by his bedside, grieved over how "awful" Casey looks while he lay unconscious and hooked up to a breathing tube, before confiding to Morgan and Chuck, "I don't even know him, but I already love him so much." Later, Casey barely manages a whisper: "You're here." And after presenting him with a bonsai tree and making a joke, Alex continues to speak with watery eyes, strained features, and a quavering voice: "Listen, I, ah,...I kind of like having my dad around. I don't just like it. I've kind of gotten used to it. So, I spent most of my life thinking that my dad was dead, and I'm not ready to do it again, OK?" With Herculean effort, Casey slowly raises his IV-taped hand towards Alex, and she clasps it with both of her own. In a final hospital moment, while returning to his room after the birth of Baby Clara, Casey informs Morgan that Alex went home, only for Alex to reappear around a corner. "No I didn't," she corrects him. "Just went to get a coffee. Whether you like it or not, Dad, I am not going anywhere." With a thoughtful purse of the lips, Casey quietly meets her vow: "Neither am I." And though he has just refused Morgan's help in wheeling back to his room, he betrays no qualms in accepting Alex's offer.

As the fallen bearing wall in Morocco suggests, the process of Casey's emotional evolution does not come without its tougher moments of entrapment. At one point, Casey considers, at Morgan's urging, reentering Alex's mother's life as well (vs. the Seduction Impossible). That is, until he finds out Katherine has moved on with another man and

Alex is uncomfortable with the idea. Pained by the necessary distance this will require him to maintain in his relationship with Alex, Casey actually broaches the subject with Chuck in what is itself a distinct moment of transparency (vs. the CAT Squad). While Chuck peruses CIA files in hopes of reconciling Sarah's relationship with a former CAT Squad friend, Casey, without solicitation, muses, "It would be nice to be like you: want to fix everything. Not now. Grimes suggested I approach Alex's mom. I was tempted at first, but she's moved on. So…I'll let it lie." But Casey finds himself caught again when he discovers the invitation to Alex's graduation Morgan receives on the table at home (vs. the Family Volkoff). When Morgan explains the awkward dynamic, Casey admits, "Stupid of me to think otherwise."

Casey's love for Alex ultimately leads him to insist she not be caught between her parents as well. When an apologetic Alex shows up at the Buy More to explain the invitation situation, Casey graciously tries to cut the matter off by saying, "Not an issue." However, Alex persists in arranging to meet him for drinks between the ceremony and dinner. Visibly conflicted, Casey makes it clear he doesn't want to be "an intrusion" or force her to lie, but when she pleads with him, he cannot decline. That is until discussing the prenup crisis with Sarah on a subsequent mission. When Sarah vents, "Hardest place for a kid is right in the middle," torn between two parents, Casey replies, "Roger that." Thus, upon his return, Casey reverses course. Even though Alex argues "lying to [Mom] kind of goes with our territory," especially "if I get to have you in my life," Casey insists, "I mind….It's not fair" and promises dinner with her the day after graduation.

Of course, Casey and Alex climb past the residual rubble of his unguarded heart as they grow increasingly comfortable with each other. Christmases will include gifts like the Mr. Pippers bear, given with an even more precious verbal gift: "I love you." Movie nights will become a weekly staple, a commitment underscored by Casey's willingness to watch "Downton Abbey," despite the absence of bombs and gunfire, and the grace to joke about the fury that will arise over the misplacement of dinner forks. Casey also reveals he has a friend--OK a girlfriend--that he would like the intrigued Alex to meet sometime. And Casey seems lukewarm about the less violent, cyber-oriented direction of Carmichael Industries only until reminded Alex will worry less. Casey even declines

Verbanski's invitation to join her in Dresden, citing two months as too long to be away from home. As he promised, he's sticking around.

In the end, Casey succeeds in integrating Alex into his life, enriching his own in the process. And he encourages others to learn from his experience. Notably, when Devon suffers from the shakes prior to the birth of Baby Clara, Casey advises, "Listen, don't make the same mistake I did. I missed my daughter's birth. Missed her whole damn childhood.... There's not a day that goes by I don't regret that. Now you get in there" (vs. the Push Mix).

CHAPTER **16:**

All Roads Lead to Home

"She let her guard down, and I want to know why." Intrigued by the striking transformation of Ryker's "loner" and Graham's "wild card," Jack Burton crosses a continent in Season 4 to investigate his daughter's motives (vs. the Wedding Planner). Jack's not the only parent scratching his head. When finally reunited with her daughter in Season 5, Emma spends some time trying to grasp the wedding pictures decorating the home of the new Mrs. Chuck Bartowski (vs. the Baby). And when Sarah walks through the door, Emma eventually asks a pointed question: "Joining the CIA and giving up everything you did, did you ever think it would lead you here?" Watching Chuck play on the floor with precious Molly, Sarah sighs and cocks her head before replying. "No. No," she smiles, "but a…Chuck's taught me that every now and then it's OK to be surprised."

As her legal maiden name suggests, Sarah Walker's journey to vulnerability and home-building is a slow and winding pilgrimage. After Sarah takes the decisive step of pursuing a real relationship with Chuck in Season 3, a decision followed by no serious detours, obstacles still loom in her path. However, the internal walls raised by years of con jobs, hotel rooms, and parental disappointment increasingly shrink to a series of smaller hurdles that Sarah succeeds in clearing, with the significant assistance of a little patience and humor from Handler Chuck. And with each tentative step she takes, Sarah reverses an initial hesitancy to actually lead the way.

At first, Sarah balks at Chuck's invitation to move in to his apartment (vs. the Role Models). Instinctively, Sarah, who betrays no moral qualms with the idea, indelicately counters, "Why would I want to do that?" before adding, "We're not a normal couple, so why do we need to pretend we have a normal life?" A curious response from a woman who has just told Casey she is willing to quit the spy life and run if necessary, explaining, "Look, no matter how much I want to be a spy, I want Chuck more....I can't risk it" (vs. The Honeymooners). Sarah even seems to double down when Chuck has at least temporarily let go of the idea. While on the mission observing the Turners (vs. the Role Models), Sarah redirects an innocent, amorous gesture from Chuck to ask, "You're not going to ask me to move in with you again, are you?" Evidently the matter occupies Sarah's mind more than Chuck's.

By episode's end, and without further pressure from Chuck, Sarah's rethinking becomes clear when she surprises him with her desire to fix up "our place" before cleaning up the Woodcomb's tiger-ravaged apartment, "That is if the offer still stands." While setting out their keepsake photos on a mantle, Sarah finally lowers her guard with her real-world avatar: "I'm sorry I freaked out when you asked me to move in with you...It's just, you know how I grew up: I spent my life in hotel rooms under fake names. I've been trained to survive a thousand situations in the field, but...no one ever taught me how to have a normal life." When Chuck, sighing, voices his doubt that they will ever be a normal couple, Sarah divulges even a bit more, admitting, "Well, I'd like to have something to fall back on when my spy life is over."

In the very next episode, Sarah ironically backs away from articulating her love for Chuck, even though she privately acknowledges her feelings for him in her video log as early as Season 2. And though one may think that she said the Three Words to a drunken Chuck cradling his faux guitar in Season Three, Sarah actually only answered "yes" to Chuck's question whether she loved him. "Vs. the Tooth" opens with Chuck and Sarah snuggling on the couch while surfing TV channels. Glimpses of buildings blowing up, rows of cars to be jumped, and laundry tumbling in a dryer flicker across the screen, foreshadowing the inner tumult Sarah evidences in her inability to reply to Chuck's simple "I love you" when he tells her moments later. Tight-lipped, Sarah smiles, breathes in deeply, and tenderly caresses his face. And though she proceeds to swallow with emotion and purse her lips, she verbalizes nothing before returning her attention back to the screen.

Chuck, visibly disappointed, falls asleep, only to dream of Sarah telling him she loves him. In his waking hours, Chuck tries to ignore the issue, but when ordered to see CIA psychiatrist Dr. Leo Dreyfuss, due to his bizarre nightmares thought to be caused by the Intersect's interaction with his subconscious, Chuck is forced to confront his angst. Sort of. After initially asserting he is happy with his girlfriend, Chuck admits, "You know she's a little distant; she could be a little more communicative...; she doesn't exactly say 'I love you' back; I know that she loves me; I'm just kind of noting it, 'cuz I know, I know that she loves me...I know that." Dreyfuss's follow-up cuts straight to the point: "Do you?"

As Chuck's condition seemingly deteriorates, he becomes institutionalized. This rocks Sarah's world. Suddenly aware of a gaping void, Sarah makes a desperate evening visit to the home of Dr. Dreyfuss and struggles to maintain a semblance of control. In the ensuing exchange, Dreyfuss uses the information gleaned from his session with Chuck to good effect:

Sarah:	You don't understand; he's not like other people. He is...incredibly special.
Dreyfuss:	Especially to you, I gather.
Sarah:	He needs to be OK....I, I need him to be OK. I'd like to go to the hospital tonight and talk to him, try and figure this out and...help him somehow, you know?...Please....I love him....
Dreyfuss:	Ever tell him that?
Sarah:	Please....please, Dr.,... I am begging you.

Not typical Sarah language. As it turns out, Chuck, not as far gone as everyone feared, is honorably returned to duty. But with a caveat: the Intersect may ultimately overwhelm his mind. Encouraged by Dreyfuss to discuss the matter with Sarah, Chuck returns home resolved to do just that. Before he can, however, Sarah interrupts, indicating she has reached a resolution of her own: "I love you....It shouldn't have taken me this long to say it, but I've never felt this way....Before you, the only future I could think about was my next mission, and now...all I can think about is a future with you.... I love you, Chuck." Overwhelmed and relieved, Chuck can't follow through with revealing his own truth.

The next obstacle in line proves Sarah's hesitancy to view her residence in Chuck's apartment as permanent. Despite choking up while revealing to Chuck, "You're my home...You always have been," Sarah finds herself unable to unpack her suitcase for weeks if not months after moving in with Chuck (vs. the Suitcase). Morgan is the first to comment on her "weird unpacking thing," but Chuck awkwardly reiterates the sentiment when assuring Sarah that he accepts her for who she is in the moments prior to a bomb exploding. But when it doesn't detonate, the combustible vibe between them remains. Matters don't improve when, later in the mission, they observe the fully unpacked hotel closet of spy model Sofia Stepanova.

Back home, Chuck finds Sarah placing a dress on the closet rack, but steps in to stop her and even takes the dress off the rack to place it back in the suitcase. "Don't unpack. Please," he pleads. "If you do it now, it's only going to be because we were talking about it, and I don't want you to do it because of that; I want you to do it when you feel comfortable here, when you feel at home." Sarah's response is sincere: "I do feel comfortable here. It's just...It doesn't come naturally to me, putting roots down." Patiently guiding Sarah into the normal world, Chuck puts her at ease. "I know. You were always on the run with your dad...and being a spy doesn't make it easy to...make a home anywhere....But I love you because we're different. And one dress is not going to make or break us."

For the moment, the matter is dropped. But after returning to Castle from the successful Paris Fashion Week mission, Sarah pointedly foreshadows a change of heart, saying, "It feels good to be home." Further accenting this forthcoming new lifestyle, Chuck, unaware of Sarah's plan, pointedly walks in to the bedroom with two bottles of water and announces, "Tonight we're going sparkling!" But his attention is immediately diverted to Sarah, doing her best Vanna White imitation at the closet door while making her own announcement, a proud smile spread across her face. "It's official." Grasping her meaning, his eyes guided by her gesture to racks full of her clothes, Chuck begins, "Oh, you didn't have to," but Sarah cuts him off. "I wanted to. I've never had a real home, and I wanted this to feel like one." Convinced she really means it, this time Chuck steps in to help. And after the tender moment centered on the photo she keeps in her suitcase "at all times," Chuck reaches for her face and kisses Sarah…before playfully throwing her on the bed while, once again, safely lifting the moment into laughter.

No sooner has this hurdle been cleared, though, when another immediately pops up in its place. After sharing an intimate moment snuggling in the wake of Sarah's unpacking milestone, Chuck, at Sarah's urging, reveals, "We have a real future…ahead of us." All is dreamily well until Chuck opens his mouth again: "Maybe Awesome's right. Marriage. Baby. Who knows? Maybe we're next." Cue the tension theme: the moment is fractured when Sarah, facing away from Chuck, ends the episode sporting a wide-eyed stare as strained as the one seen through apartment window in the Season 1 finale or the fountain break-up in "vs. The Break-up," minus the glassy eyes.

Despite Sarah's admonition and his agreement to "take things slow" (vs. the Cubic Z), Chuck subsequently feels compelled to improve their communication skills by initiating conversations recommended in Dr. Fred Hornblower's 101 Conversations Before 'I Do' (vs. the Coup D'état). Predictably, Sarah asks Chuck, "Why do we always have to talk and push and change things? Why can't we just be? What if we do 'I Do' and it changes us?" As circumstances have it, their predicament mirrors the strained relationship they encounter on their next mission between the Costa Gravan premier and his wife of 25 years, who claims their love has changed from their revolutionary days. The dialogue of this argument held at pistol point drips with dramatic irony. Picking up on the wife's accusation, Sarah only adds to the tension of the moment by asserting, "So, change ruined things!" only for Chuck to counter, "But change is unavoidable. Unavoidable! Life is full of changes. Constantly changing. And the question is, no matter what the changes are, is the love still there?" Ultimately and ironically, Sarah, converted by Chuck's argument, steps in to diffuse the crisis by tentatively suggesting, "Uh, that love, that you had in the cave: that doesn't have to change," while meeting Chuck's eyes.

Safely snuggled in bed back in Echo Park, Sarah proceeds to actually use one of Dr. Hornblower's techniques at the end of the episode. Believing Chuck asleep, Sarah elects to talk about her issue with her partner while he, facing away from her, supposedly slumbers: "I love you, Chuck. Nothing's ever gonna change that. And if you asked me for real, then my answer…would be 'yes.'" For a moment, Sarah silently contemplates her words, as if even she can hardly absorb them, before the lens focuses on Chuck's subtle but pleased smirk, symmetrically rounding off her privately freaked response to his bedtime words in "vs. the Suitcase."

In a few more episodes, ironically, Sarah will prove so intent on making her delayed engagement become a reality that she will transform into a rogue she-male while crossing the planet to rescue Chuck (see Chapter 14: Phase Three). And after the engagement does become a reality, Sarah will deflect her father's concerns with confidence. With Sarah's wedding just weeks away (vs. the Wedding Planner), Jack confesses, "Truth is, I never thought my little girl would settle down. I thought you'd end up more like me: Just one adventure after another.... Isn't that what you want?" Without a hint of conflict, Sarah replies, "It was…but um…I found a home here..a good one, and I'm happy." And by the time she speaks her wedding vows, Sarah will not only intimate, "…I want to spend and learn and love the rest of my life with you," but she won't even let Morgan fully verbalize the vow before affirming, "I do."

Sarah's resolve to tie the knot with Chuck doesn't necessarily translate into a willingness to do it with public fanfare, at least not at first. Thus, a conflict linked to the marriage issue surrounds the question of elopement, which Sarah prefers, or the big family wedding that Chuck prefers (vs. the Seduction Impossible). Sarah's initial concern, as it turns out, is only part of the issue. Claiming "your family is going to be… intense until we get married," a charge that Chuck does not refute, Sarah wishes to "run away to some beautiful…romantic, amazing place [where] all of this stress and pressure could be avoided." After verbally unloading on Chuck, she pointedly steps behind him to check the breach of a pistol on the gun rack while checking his reaction over her shoulder.

Though Chuck waits a day or two to formally respond, when he does, he makes it clear he has no desire to elope, "not one bit." Not to be deterred, both Chuck and Sarah begin a Roan Montgomery-like seduction to manipulate the other to their position, thus the episode title's double entendre. Chuck comes home dressed like an elegant spy, even as Sarah appears modeling a belly dancer outfit she said she would never wear. Though sternly tested, Chuck confronts Sarah about her seduction technique, and when she points out his, Chuck says his just isn't working as well.

Beckman's call to a mission interrupts matters, but by the time they reach Morocco again the real communication finally continues. When asking about the cons of a big wedding, Sarah finally fesses up to the deeper issue involved: "Who am I gonna invite? Who's gonna come? Who's gonna walk me down the aisle?" Chagrined by his insensitivity, Chuck profusely apologizes, as does Sarah for concealing her genuine concerns. This leads Chuck to overcompensating with his emotional baggage handling. When Sarah stonewalls his offer to help with her family issues, Chuck secretly and naively invites the CAT Squad to the engagement party. By the end of an episode filled with awkwardness due to overstepping his bounds (vs. the CAT Squad), Chuck ends up being sent home by Sarah to struggle with her gal pals' baggage simply so that he will leave hers alone.

Still, when she reconciles with her former partners, who come to the engagement party and plan to become bridesmaids, Sarah is left fingering her ring in the bedroom mirror. In contrast to the image from "vs. the Honeymooners," when she simply stared at their impromptu rings in the mirror on the train, Sarah's handling the ring on her finger in her bedroom suggests that her approaching wedding and married life is beginning to feel more tangible if not yet entirely real. And after telling Chuck, "…Don't ever stop helping me…There are a thousand [other] ways I need your help every single day," Sarah is ready to sincerely say, "Let's party."

Sarah's reversal on the formal wedding issue completes itself when Ellie steps in to help. The newly minted matron of honor, based on her own experience, tells a skeptical Sarah there will come a moment when the wonder of her approaching marriage will hit her (vs. the First Bank of Evil); she just needs to find the specific element that will spark it. At first nothing, not flowers, invitations, or colors, seems to engage Sarah's interest. But even to Ellie's surprise, Sarah eventually responds enthusiastically to the suggestion of searching for the dress she will wear: "Yeah, yeah. I've been looking for a way to ease into this, and I think this may be it. In fact, I'm going to go do some research right now." Using Castle's fantasy mission attire collection, Sarah proceeds to unleash her inner bride, trying on a slew of dresses…until one leaves her momentarily speechless. Finding her voice, Sarah whispers to herself, "Oh my God…It's perfect." Looking at the holographic wedding couple nearby, she smiles. "We're getting married." Her hands meet over her nose; her jaw drops. "Oh my God," she gasps with a wide smile, "We're getting married?" Tears begin to well up as she bites her lower lip. Reality has finally hit home.

And the feeling lingers. During the subsequent bank heist mission in Macao, Chuck asks about the dress, and the lady in the cat suit holding the machine gun gushes, "Well, it's actually really pretty, and I never thought I would say this, but...I felt like a princess." From there, it's on to deciding whether to fly the wedding cake in from France and reserve a private island for the ceremony. By the time they write the check, Sarah's wedding plans will total $26,000 (vs. the Wedding Planner). If the viewer needed any further convincing, it comes when Chuck and Sarah arrive to a magical courtyard decorated by Ellie (vs. the Last Details). Both are overwhelmed for a moment before Chuck recovers and asks, "Are you ready for this?" Without hesitation, Sarah looks into Chuck's eyes with certainty: "Absolutely!"

In the middle of all this wedding planning, Sarah encounters another temporary roadblock: the prenup to protect the money she has set aside in case her dad runs into more trouble with the law (vs. the Family Volkoff). The irony is that she expects Chuck to want to talk about it with her and then is disappointed when he takes the advice of Casey and Morgan to "just be cool" and sign it with no questions asked. Uncharacteristically, Sarah keeps bringing up the "non-issue" with Chuck in the middle of missions, alternatively assuring him, "Look, Chuck, a prenup doesn't mean the end of our marriage," and, "It's just....family stuff" that's "got nothing to do with us." Suddenly a paragon of understanding, Chuck ironically ends up assuring Sarah, "Well look, hey, you're a spy, and spies have secrets they need to protect. It's cool." In a complete turnabout, Sarah begins to argue against her own position: "No. I, I don't keep secrets from you." Eventually, Sarah resorts to asking, "....Don't you want to know why I asked you to sign it?" Chuck still won't bite, answering, "I figured you'd tell me when you were ready." Ultimately, Chuck's unquestioning trust wins the argument without a fight. While looking through binoculars outside the cave in the Swiss alps, signifying her new clarity of vision, Sarah tells Casey, "...Now I see what Chuck's side of it would have been like....flipping out about a relationship based on the contents of an envelope. (Pause.) Seeing the end before we've even started."

By the time they arrive home, Sarah acts on her epiphany. Seated on the couch next to Chuck, her knees drawn up as in other intimate scenes, Sarah tears up the document and begs, "Please forget that that ever existed, OK?" However, Chuck throws her another curve. Turning to face her, he pulls out his own prenup. A bit miffed, she pulls out the handwritten sheet, frown on her face, and begins to read aloud in a legal monotone: "I, Sarah Walker, promise to (sigh)…always love Chuck Bartowski …." A smile begins to form on her face. "And in return, he will always love me." Then the laughter begins. "I can't read this fine print." Looking into the distance, Chuck continues, "The fine print says, 'I promise Chuck I will not even contemplate the word 'divorce,' and I will never use my prenup." When Chuck notes he's already signed it, Sarah's only response is a relentless smile as she gladly accepts a pen.

Perhaps Sarah's most dramatic reversal features the issue of motherhood. The viewer may recall that Sarah's freaked response at the close of "vs. the Suitcase" is to more than just marriage: the kids part rankles her even more. This response seems particularly ironic given that, almost three years earlier (vs. the Crown Vic), the topic already occupies her mind when asking Casey, "Do you ever just want to have a normal life? Have a family? Children?" Initially, Sarah plays it close to the vest, preferring to take her angst out on her sparring partner, Casey, while asking him pointed questions about how parenthood has affected him (vs. the Cubic Z). Then she makes a confession: "I'm a spy. I can't even process the idea of having kids right now…." Sarah plans to have a chat with Chuck, but the moment vanishes when the unexpected prisoner transfer involving Heather Chandler and Hugo Panzer requires their attention. When the next opportunity avails itself, Sarah places her gun and ammo in their respective pre-formed locations in the foam case even as she metaphorically struggles to put her feelings in place. However, before she is able to voice them, Chuck flashes on Heather's involvement with Frost, and the opportunity again vanishes.

Instead, she spends the night being "poked" on the sensitive topic when Chandler realizes they are a couple and needles them. "So, how deep are you? Shacking up? Doing the dog thing first, or straight to babies? One? Five?" In a classic case of projection, Sarah advises Chuck, "If you let her get under your skin about the living together thing, and about the other thing that she mentioned, we're not going to get anywhere." In fact,

Sarah's inability to even name the "other thing" recalls her denial of the kiss of Chuck in Season 1, which she insisted on calling The Incident.

The escape of Panzer leads to Sarah guarding the snarky Chandler all night, much of it in the air vents of the Buy More. Chandler takes every opportunity to get a rise out of her counterpart, telling Chuck, "She's all spy. White weddings? Rug rats and a mini-van? It's not in her wiring." But when Sarah finally has a private moment with her nemesis, Sarah speaks her mind: "You don't know who I am or what I want or the thoughts in my head. We have nothing in common." As she leaves, Chandler admits maybe she is wrong about Sarah; that maybe Sarah really is "capable of vulnerability" and that Chuck "seems like a really nice guy," adding, "And he's really in love. Are you?" Sarah only replies, "Goodbye, Heather," but after Sarah turns and walks away, she takes a last glance back at Chandler that indicates the answer is in fact yes.

With the prisoners gone, the time for Sarah's chat with Chuck finally arrives, and so does the time for Sarah's quiet transparency. "The other night when you repeated what Awesome said about having kids: it scared me." Assured by Chuck that Sarah is "nothing like" Chandler, Sarah counters, "For a long time, I was exactly like her." But when she continues, Sarah's words subtly accent her internal rebirth: "…It took me a night in the guts of the building to realize that I'm not anymore. At all. And I don't want to be…But I do need to take things slow." On cue, the good humor man arrives with just the right words to put Sarah at ease: "…Who am I kidding? I'm barely on solid food myself." Even mid-way through Season 4 (vs. the Seduction Impossible), both Chuck and Sarah still beg Beckman for a mission to escape the family intensity of Baby Clara mania.

Fast forward a year, and the emotional landscape looks vastly different (vs. the Kept Man). After a pregnancy 'scare,' Sarah, and Chuck, too, are "relieved" to find the test result negative, but they voice their feelings with generally downcast expressions and at best tight-lipped smiles decidedly lacking in enthusiasm. Indeed, even before admitting relief, Sarah claims to feel "strange," and Chuck agrees. Was it really a scare, then? Perhaps not. Chuck's repetition of "It's changing, it's changing, it's changing," spoken in regards to the results of the test indicator in his hand, seems to also indicate their shifting feelings about starting a family.

At episode's end, this conflicted response becomes more explicit. Chuck wakes up to find Sarah, unable to sleep, on the computer ready to make "a small confession." Showing him the boys' names she has been researching online, she reveals, "Part of me was kind of hoping I was pregnant....I mean, it's not like I want a baby right this second, but it's not the worst idea in the world." In agreement, Chuck shakes his head before speaking. "Listen to us talking about kids and a house and a real family. Did you ever think we'd ever be talking about stuff like this?" This time, Sarah provides the humor. "Nope! Especially not with such a huge nerd."

As Sarah nears the end of her personal pilgrimage, she arrives at a crossroads that always lurked in the distance and was postponed at least once at the end of Season 2: leaving the spy life for a family-friendly one. Chuck is the first to voice his qualms with the status quo in Season 5 (vs. the Business Trip). Worried about his hunted best friend, "his brain almost turned to mush," and their ban from the CIA, he muses, "I just wonder what it would be like to be a normal married couple: regular 9 to 5's, more taco nights, less evil cabals." At this point, Sarah's muted response signals she's in no hurry to holster her pistol. However, the issue clearly stays on her mind, as evidenced in her exchange with Verbanski in "vs. the Hack Off."

As they penetrate The Collective base, Sarah initiates a personal conversation, ostensibly to encourage her female colleague to open up about her feelings for Casey. The topic, though, turns towards Sarah's future when Verbanski can't see herself ever putting a family ahead of work. Sounding like the Sarah of old, Verbanski confides, "I've been doing this since I was 16 years old; I've never had another job, not in my entire life. I wouldn't know what to do if I did." Then she turns the spotlight on Sarah: "How about you? Would you do anything else?" Before Sarah, pondering, can answer, some bad guys need taking out.

Part of Sarah's issue revolves around Verbanski's similar concern with the unknown. When Chuck suggests Carmichael Industries should shift from a tech company to a spy company, Sarah nervously asks, "What would my job be at Carmichael Industries? I mean...what would I do?"(vs. the Hack Off). And when Chuck briefly reverses himself, claiming, "We've got to be the best spies we've ever been" to deal with the very real threat Decker's quest for vengeance presents to their lives, he gets no argument from Sarah. But when they succeed in emerging from the Decker/Shaw arc back in the good graces of the CIA, it is Sarah, not Chuck, who urges putting the Dream House on hold and retaining a bit of control over their lives (vs. the Baby), explaining, "I gave my life to the CIA for a really long time...and I chose it over my family and my friends, and that was the right thing for me to do at the time. But...I'm different now. You know, things have changed...You've changed me. (Inhale.) I don't want to go back."

In short order, though, simply saying no to the CIA isn't enough for Sarah, who concludes that all traditional spy work proves incongruent with raising a family. While on a mission in the Florida Everglades rescuing Verbanski (vs. the Kept Man), Sarah displays trouble focusing on the task at hand, asking, "What if we had a baby relying on us to come home...and something happened?...Who would raise the kids? What, what would happen to them?" The final straw comes when Sarah prowls the apartment, gun in hand, after hearing the newspaper boy throw a paper against the door (vs. Bo). Without further discussion, Sarah, not Chuck, insists, "I want to quit spying." After informing Chuck she's "been up all night...thinking about our futures and...maybe babies," Sarah reveals, "Look, I'm a spy, and that's all I ever thought that I could be, but I realized we don't have to give up what we've already built." Sarah then reveals a new Carmichael Industries concept: "Countering cyber terrorism," a tech firm "but more spied up, so we keep your computer know-how and mix it with my experience in international bad-guyery." The pistol is about to go into the holster.

Reaching the end of the road home, Sarah balks at the Dream House on the beach in favor of something more "cozy, homey, and simple" (vs. the Zoom). Chuck, confused over exactly what Sarah would like when she doesn't seem thrilled with the one he found on the beach, tells her that instead of "playing detective and trying to read her mind" she should just tell him. Still not entirely comfortable expressing her most intimate thoughts even at the start of Season 5, Sarah informs him, "...This isn't something that I've ever told anybody." After Chuck reminds her that husbands are privileged to know such secrets, Sarah takes one more step in vulnerability. "Uh...well, when I was a little girl, my..uh..dad's 'work' kept us moving around a lot, and I..(inhale, sigh) always imaged what a real family would feel like, you know, with the perfect home for us all would be." Feeling "stupid," Sarah needs additional encouragement before completing her revelation. "Well, I always.. imagined a little white house with a red door and—don't laugh— but it had a picket fence just like…you know the houses you see on TV that people live in." When Chuck calls it "perfect," Sarah turns her head to him, her eyes searching his. "Really?" Really.

When he finds the house, Chuck proclaims it "perfect," largely because of a door frame (vs. the Baby). He proceeds to explain to his wife, whose itinerate childhood makes the point difficult to grasp, that it can be used to measure the growth of their kids each year, just as he and Ellie were. Sarah agrees. "I want this house, and I want the life you have envisioned for us. I want every single part of it." And after the significant interruption of the mission involving protecting Molly from Ryker, Chuck and Sarah return for a candlelit evening in the Dream House they suddenly can't afford. Chuck, perhaps still a bit chagrined, knowing the signing bonus with the CIA could serve as the down payment, trades places with Sarah, who takes the torch for their future. Taking out a knife, she walks to the door frame and starts carving, to Chuck's initial consternation. "You know we don't own this home." Undeterred, Sarah continues carving while speaking. "I know….but we will. One day. It might not be tomorrow or the next day. And it may take us months or years of hard work, but one day this will all be ours….And when it is, I would like to always remember this moment." Looking with satisfaction at her handiwork, she turns and looks up to Chuck, extending the knife and a challenge to him. "So what do you say? Are you still in?" Shaking his head with a grin, he follows her lead.

Sarah meant what she said. Every single part of it. Forced to download the Intersect glasses in a moment of dire need (vs. Bo), she is confronted with a tantalizing temptation. After "chilling" on the Bullet Train, phrasing that foregrounds the brief but tangible tension in the air as they face one another, Chuck finally cracks the ice and asks Sarah about her experience with the Intersect. With her face lit up, she quickly confesses, "You know, I've been a spy for so long, and I've never felt this powerful in my entire life. It's incredible" (vs. the Bullet Train). This leaves Chuck wondering. "Are you ready to say goodbye to all of it?"

Though the lure may have proven too much for her at an earlier time, Sarah is too far down the road home to turn back now. "I don't want to live my life in danger anymore," she confirms, smiling. "I'm ready to retire and start a family. Our future is exciting enough." With a pleased grin, Chuck responds with a bit of innuendo: "We have some time…and starting a family is not something you can just jump right into." Some minutes later, they lie dreamily, propped up in the compartment's micro bed. Assuring him she hasn't forgotten anything, despite her use of the Intersect glasses, Sarah instructs Chuck to include the picket fence on the Dream House he sketches. But Chuck proves her 'wrong.' Upon his adding the baby missing from Sarah's arms, Sarah echoes Chuck's whisper, "Some day."

CHAPTER 17:

Missing Links

It's a quiet day at the Woodcomb's. Devon sits on the couch reading to a wide-eyed Baby Clara, his face hidden behind the book's cover (vs. the Family Volkoff). However, the text, discussing "missing links" and fossil specimens "in a state of intermediary development," isn't a children's story but Richard Leakey's *Origins: The Emergence and Evolution of Our Species and its Possible Future*. The anthropological study perfectly figures the woman framed over Devon's shoulder as he reads: Ellie Bartowski Woodcomb. Initially a fairly flat character, Ellie evidences intermediary development as the series progresses, evolving into a textured woman who restores missing links and enjoys a possibility-filled future by its conclusion.

The origin of Ellie's character is best understood within the context of her abandonment by parents at a young age due to reasons beyond her initial frame of reference. In one sense, this leaves the pointed winner of a neurology fellowship with an almost neurotic sense of responsibility for her younger and fellow-orphaned sibling. Before her father, Stephen Bartowski, himself disappears one morning after promising to make her pancakes, he charges the already motherless Ellie with looking out for Chuck. While settling a quarrel over their mother's broken bracelet in a flashback to their childhood (vs. the Ring: Part II), he tells his daughter, "I know it's hard, El, but your brother does have a knack for getting into trouble. But you, you're going to have to protect Chuck. Be there for him no matter what. 'Cuz you're his big sister. Can you do that for me?" After a long pause, she promises.

In early seasons, Ellie fulfills this promise in benign and even comical ways. During their childhood, she informed Chuck that Peaches II, the family dog, ran away rather than reveal it was hit by a car, a claim she maintains to a crestfallen adult Chuck while playing The Newlywed Game despite Morgan's assertion (vs. the Wookiee). Speaking of "Organ," Ellie spends three plus seasons worrying about the effect of the Bearded One on her brother…and trying to keep her own distance from his lingering amorous affections. When it comes to Chuck's romantic life, Ellie repeatedly displays angst over his inability to get over Bryce Larkin stealing Jill at Stanford. The birthday party opening the series, intended to introduce Chuck to eligible bachelorettes, fails miserably due to his penchant for musing over Jill. Afterwards, Ellie repeats a "rehearsed" speech: "Stanford was five years ago. You need to move on. It's time." And each time Chuck does find a new girl, Big Sis shows sheer rapture. For his first cover date with Sarah, she insists on picking Chuck's outfit and coaches him on the "old girlfriend rule." With slight variation, the dynamic repeats with Hannah when Ellie discovers the relationship while spying on the Buy More video room and makes her acquaintance next morning in Chuck's apartment while Hannah drips in a bath towel.

On a more serious level, Ellie, unaware of Chuck's moonlighting with the CIA, agonizes over her perception of Chuck's professional under-achievement. Thinking him overqualified for his job at the Nerd Herd desk and unmotivated to move forward with his life, she repeatedly challenges him to think bigger. When Chuck covers for his late night returns from missions with tales of playing video games, Ellie disagrees with Devon's take of harmlessly "blowing off steam," arguing, "One night has a funny way of adding up," and adding it was "cool when you're in college…" (vs. Tom Sawyer). After Chuck dismisses finishing his college classes with claims he has a lot on his plate, Ellie challenges him: "Like what, precisely? …Shouldn't your life be moving…somewhere?"

Ellie proves so concerned she secretly arranges a meeting with Sarah to confess, "…It's like he's slipping back into Old Chuck mode….No confidence, no direction. It's, it's the Morgan years revisited." Agonizing over how Chuck is "twelve credits short of a real life," Ellie admits, "I know that I sound like his mother. Just tell me that I don't have anything to worry about, and I will lay off." Matters repeat themselves when Chuck returns from Prague a failed spy (vs. the Pink Slip). After an initial grace period, Ellie asks her bath-robed, cheese ball-chomping brother, "Got a game plan? Job Hunting?" Days and weeks pass, and when a newly returned Morgan doesn't succeed either, Ellie bursts: "All right, Chuck!

That is enough! Sit up! You are getting off this couch and you are going to do something today!"

Most significantly, Ellie stays awake at night wondering what life will be like if her only remaining link to family, Chuck, goes missing as well. Chuck's survival proves paramount in Season 3 when she comes to the realization that he has lived a double life for years without her knowledge, much of it in harm's way. Ellie can't help being offended as "the last person to know" when Chuck's real identity as a CIA operative is revealed in conjunction with their father being murdered by Shaw and The Ring (vs. the Ring: Part II). Of course, she still risks tailing the armored car that carries her brother along with Sarah and Casey to their seeming deaths and panics when she loses contact. And when reunited with Chuck, after Team Bartowski heroically and accidentally foils Shaw's execution plan, she runs to Chuck, unable to contain the relief in her embrace. Still, Ellie only pledges her support for the effort to take Shaw and The Ring down on one condition: "Chuck, I made a promise to protect you, but I can't do it, not from this. So you finish it, and then you're done" (vs. The Ring: Part II). When Chuck resists, Ellie insists, "We are all that we have left, Chuck. And I'm not going to lose you, too." Meaning business, Ellie proceeds to confirm Chuck's pledge on two more occasions before the close of the episode.

Ellie's fear of losing Chuck causes her to continue to insist on this stance even when she gains a new appreciation for what leaving the CIA supposedly cost Chuck. After Sarah's and his heroics in Costa Grava save the Woodcombs at Premier Goya's gala, she tells him, "You were pretty good at that spy stuff, weren't you?...You just seemed so...alive back there. I don't think I really realized what you were giving up for me" (vs. the Coup D'état). Having resumed his spy activities without her knowledge, Chuck plays it down, saying, "I didn't really give up all that much." But Ellie replies, "Yes you did. And it must have been difficult. And I just wanted to tell you that I'm so glad you have a life now that we can talk about. No secrets. Especially now with the baby, you being the only family on my side...." And a year later, when Ellie senses she may yet lose Chuck, she lurks in the Buy More after Chuck instructs her to go home. As a result, she saves Chuck by knocking out Shaw, who is so desperate in defeat that he resorts to using a gun (vs. the Santa Suit). Ellie then makes her motive clear: "That man took our father away from us, Chuck. I wasn't going to let him take anybody else."

Ellie's abandonment also leads to struggles restoring links with her absentee parents when the opportunities arise. In Season 2, she confides to Chuck that though she wasn't one to dream about her wedding while growing up, "one thing was clear: that Dad would walk me down the aisle...," further admitting, "It's just really hard to let that go" (vs. the Sensei). That spurs Chuck's quest to find him for Ellie, but when he succeeds, the reunion doesn't get off to an ideal start. Ellie's initial response to Dad walking in the door brings out the latent sting of her betrayal: "Pancakes?...You said you were going to make pancakes" (vs. the Dream Job). Confessing to Chuck, "I'm just so mad at him," after he follows her into her bedroom, Ellie asks, "Aren't you mad at him?" "I was," he responds, "But then I realized...we can either choose to hate him for the rest of our lives or choose to forgive him." Though Ellie initially claims, "It's easier to hate him," she changes her mind when Chuck observes, "...He's all we've got left, El. This could be our last chance to be a family again."

After an uncomfortable afternoon, Ellie regroups to offer a toast to Stephen at dinner, saying, "We are extremely grateful to have you home." Still, when things go south on Chuck's first day on the job at the company of their father's rival, Ted Roark, Ellie rashly accuses her dad of "some crazy, made-up vendetta of yours." In the aftermath, Stephen soberly admits, "The only thing Ellie owes me is a few well-deserved trust issues," before telling Devon the real reason Ellie still simmers over his bachelor party is "she doesn't want you to turn into me." Similar to her limited view of Chuck, Ellie can't fathom her father's "crazy" behavior and sudden disappearances given her ignorance of his double life. Thus, when informed Stephen has left without notice, she confesses, "I thought that he would be different than that guy that walked out on us. I guess I just expected too much from him." Knowing otherwise, Chuck advises, "Don't count him out yet." In fact, after the Castle crew unites to take out Roark and Fulcrum, Ellie's father arrives in time to walk his beaming daughter down the aisle twice and promise, "I'm not going anywhere" (vs. the Ring).

Not until Season 3, however, does Ellie learn the full truth about her father's identity, a revelation that comes after she unknowingly betrays her father. Duped by The Ring into thinking she is protecting her father by revealing his whereabouts, she succeeds in making contact through the classified ads. Shrewdly, Steven shows up without notice, and when he does the family spends an evening laughing over past memories. But as events begin to unravel, including placing a bug on her father, so does Ellie's ignorance regarding her father's life. Hearing her "crazy" Dad described by Justin, a rogue Fulcrum contact, as "brilliant…in the world of molecular computing" at their meet leaves Ellie incredulous (vs. the Tooth). Ellie gains more clues after Chuck, who she also discovers is a spy, shows up later at her apartment with Stephen in tow seeking her help. Leading them to her rendezvous point with Justin, Ellie, observing her dad whispering with Chuck, demands the truth. Indeed, her last words to her father reveal Ellie's most vital missing emotional link: "I need to hear you say it. I need to know there's a reason that you left us" (vs. the Subway). But there is no time. Acknowledging "It's a long story," Stephen promises to tell it when he returns. But before he leaves, he vows, "It's the last time I'm going to walk away from you. I promise. I love you, Baby."

Alas, he never does return. Unable to remain behind at the rendez-vous bench, Ellie spies at least the aftermath of his murder from behind the subway door. Despite her devastation, Ellie is at least comforted with the knowledge that her father's absence was not personal; that it was actually necessary and intended to protect her and her brother. Moreover, Chuck affirms the story begun by Justin, confirming their dad "wasn't crazy…Our dad was a hero. He was a great man…who did amazing things. He was not perfect, not as a dad, no, but he was great….That's the secret I most wanted you to know." Ellie clearly becomes a believer in her own right in Season 4, when, after watching Chuck's Intersect demonstration with Morgan in Castle, she gawks, "Our dad was amazing" (vs. Agent X). However, even in the scene that concludes Season 3, Ellie is already able to sincerely join the toast, raising her glass before speaking: "To Dad."

Just as she must work through conflict with her absentee dad, Ellie deals with resentment regarding her mother. Her attitude is captured by the annual Mother's Day ritual she observes with Chuck, which they "celebrate" to mark the day their mom left them and they learned to take care of themselves (vs. the Sizzling Shrimp). Ellie confides to Chuck, "I hated [Mom] for leaving," especially since it left Chuck feeling like it was his fault due to breaking her necklace (vs. the Ring: Part II). And much like the approaching wedding turned Ellie's mind to her father, the approaching birth of her child increasingly turns Ellie's mind to the missing link of her mother.

While Awesome sleeps, a restless Ellie gets up in middle of night to look at photo album stored away in the closet to silently stare at childhood photos depicting her mom and dad, the void visible on her features (vs. the Suitcase). When Chuck feels compelled to reveal to Ellie his search for Mary, as well as his hope that circumstances beyond their horizon are responsible for her absence, Ellie muses, "What story can possibly explain leaving your family?... What if our mother is exactly who we think she is?" (vs. the Coup D'état). But in the space of an episode Ellie rethinks things, explaining, "I'm having a little girl, and...is she ever going to know her grandmother?" (vs. the Couch Lock).

Chuck's big sister can't help but yearn for her presence. Even as Chuck arrives with news of a reunion that will rock her world, Ellie herself points out the irony: "The mother that I wish would disappear [Honey Woodcomb] is here to answer all of my questions, and the mother that I wish I could talk to has...disappeared forever" (vs. the Aisle of Terror). The inner tension continues at the restaurant, where Ellie sips a glass of water pointedly filled with bittersweet lemon slices. Teeming with ambivalence, she asks Chuck, "So what do I do when she walks in the door? I, part of me wants to be reserved, show that I'm an adult, that I've been just fine since she left. The other part of me just wants to hug her." But on this night, she is left with only the bitter, not the sweet, when Chuck, witnessing Mary's abduction by his Castle colleagues, returns to the table to report, "...I'm sorry, but Mom is not coming." And when Ellie vents, "Why does she keep doing this to us?" he can no longer keep his remaining secret: "Because she's a spy." The slow recognition filling Ellie's face evidences her pain.

Ellie's conflicted heart is figured nowhere more intricately than in the scene hosting Mary as part of Mary's condition for revealing Chuck's location (vs. the First Fight). Ellie serves lemonade, reprising the image introduced at the restaurant and highlighting the sweet and sour moment for both. Mary walks in cuffed, signifying the status of her relationship with Ellie: not only is Mary prevented from indulging her desire for intimacy given her prolonged absence, but also even now she cannot make lasting amends given the ongoing, "complicated" nature of her Volkoff mission.

For her part, Ellie is confused over not only how to arrange her battling emotions but also how much she should protect her heart from further staining, imaged by her struggle over where to place the coasters she admits she doesn't normally use. Seeing her pain, Mary reaches out her cuffed hands to reassure her daughter even as tears start to stream down Ellie's face. Later, Mary will again use them to place a lock of hair affectionately behind her ear when leaving. The mood lightens momentarily when recalling Ellie falling asleep between her parents on long trips in the car, Ellie's vivid memory of the blue leather seats, special ordered by her dad, hinting at the comfort her parents provided as a child. But when Ellie changes the subject, asserting, "I just want to know what happened. I want to know the truth," Mary notably takes a swig of lemonade before answering. Finishing the tale, Mary confesses, "I wish that telling you that I did this all for you and Chuck made a difference, but I know it doesn't. And…" But time is up. And though Mary clearly yearns to say more before leaving, she wills herself to turn abruptly to the door, again her cuffed hands before her.

After an awkward beginning, a slightly less awkward sequel occurs (at least for Ellie) when Chuck shows up with their mom for the Thanksgiving leftovers meal with Volkoff. Given the impression that Alexei should be credited for freeing her mother from the erroneous notions of the CIA (vs. the Leftovers), Ellie is at least able to play a spirited game of charades with her mother's equally masquerading handler. Real healing does come with time, though. The next time Ellie and Mary meet, the day of Baby Clara's birth, Chuck nobly defers to his mother when only one family member can enter the birthing room. Gratefully accepting the gesture, Mary promises to let Ellie know they are all outside. And when Ellie, in the midst of labor, sees her mother walk through the door, she pauses just long enough to flash her own grateful smile and speak between breathes: "You came!" Mary takes her place beside Devon at the bedside, this time notably lacking cuffs, where Ellie earnestly reaches out to clasp the hand of the woman who will go on to become Baby Clara's devoted grandmother.

Even while restoring and preserving links within her birth family, Ellie also overcomes challenges presented in her marriage with Devon. Planning for the wedding proves the first battleground when Devon's awesome parents prove a little too controlling. Even as Ellie is introduced to Honey Woodcomb, her future mother-in-law informs her, "I just can't wait to start planning your wedding," while handing over a scrapbook full of ideas. After learning a catering tasting session is also in the works, Ellie, with visible concern, replies, "Wow, it looks like you already have!" and retreats to the kitchen to "go kill [her]self." But the fun is just starting. While registering at the Buy More, Honey assures Ellie she will need a vacuum sealer more than she thinks before moving on to choosing a camcorder. Ellie plays along nicely, but when left alone puts a bar code reader to her head and pulls the trigger.

During the caterer's tasting that evening, matters finally go too far. Ignoring Ellie's input on the cake samples, Honey says, "Oh, it doesn't matter. Let's agree on the red velvet." Husband Woody approves, also suggesting "sorbet between courses" and white ties. Most unnerving, Woody proceeds to inform Ellie he'd be "honored" to walk her down the aisle given her family situation. Even as Devon suggests tabling talk about the wedding, Ellie unloads: "I said yes to the big wedding, and I said yes to the burgundy organza bridesmaid dresses, and I.just.can't.say. yes anymore! And I'm sorry because I know you're trying to help, but the answer is 'No!'" With repeated apologies, she leaves the table…only for Honey to densely offer to answer Ellie's phone when Chuck calls.

A higher hurdle proves overcoming the unfortunate circumstances of Devon's bachelor party after its high jacking by Chuck's temporary handler, Agent Forrest, in need of his key card for a mission at the hospital (vs. the Broken Heart). A drugged Devon doesn't remember the events of the evening, but a few choice photos on Jeffster's computer screen at the Buy More fill in the details for Ellie, who is not only hurt by Devon's behavior but also Morgan's and Chuck's efforts to hide the 'truth' from her. Ironically, the sudden departure of Ellie's dad provides the opportunity for Devon, though innocent in the affair, to make meaningful amends. Pointedly cooking her pancakes, he assures Ellie, "Well, if it's any consolation, I'm not going anywhere. Ever. I mean no matter how hard things get between us. 'Cuz that's what married people do, right?" Devon can even make a joke about the party without Ellie exploding.

After the wedding, a different set of challenges awaits, including competing dreams. Partially to protect Ellie, Devon has a vision for joining Dr.'s Without Borders and heading to Africa with Ellie for an adventure. His heart is set on it when news arrives that Ellie has been accepted into the program of her dreams: a USC neurology fellowship (vs. the Tic Tac). Thus begins a battle in which the newlyweds become so desperate for personal affirmation they enlist the opinion of Morgan, who switches sides in a matter of minutes. After some soul searching, Ellie decides to put her dream on hold for the sake of her husband's. To a stunned Chuck, she confides, "...Dreams change. And if there is one thing I know for sure, it's that I want to be with Devon. And that might require some sacrifice for both of us, but...he's the best choice I ever made." Devon, having reached the same conclusion, comes to "steal" Ellie away to a house decorated with a congratulations banner and a bottle of champagne. Reversing himself, he urges, "If this is important to you, then it is important to me. I'm sorry I lost sight of that. Babe, take the job. We'll make it work, together." With a deeply pleased smile, Ellie embraces Devon. After deferring to one another, though, they end up seeking their common dream in Africa with the help of a sabbatical from the hospital.

In less exotic fashion, Ellie learns how to deal with mundane, everyday life as well. Even while engaged, Ellie and Devon struggle with keeping their romance alive. When a rushed Devon suggests hitting the shower for a quickie, Ellie informs him, "You know what? It would be nice if we had some romance on occasion" (vs. the Seduction). Explaining he has only forty two minutes before performing an emergency endotracheal intubation, Devon eventually admits, "I guess I have been remiss in the romance department" after Ellie points out they have not shared a "single romantic date since we've been engaged."

Accepting his mission, Devon proceeds to consult Morgan rather than probe Ellie for her preferences, and "the furry little bastard" purposely gives wrong answers that ruin the date. Despairing at the logistics of planning a make-up date, Devon asks, "When? I've got to be at work in twenty minutes. I have a five AM call tomorrow. I'll do it. I just hope I'm not too late." After apologizing to Ellie, Devon confesses, "I know I may seem like Mr. Smooth, but the truth is I don't have a million moves. All I know is I love you." Content with his heart, Ellie replies, "I don't need moves, Devon. Just the fact that you're trying is enough." Having a brother-in-law that shames the CIA into helping out with a home strewn with rose petals and candles doesn't hurt either.

Similar challenges lay in wait as a married couple a year later. While moving into their new apartment, Ellie picks up their wedding album and stares before asking, "Is it just me, or does it feel like a million years ago?...What happened to us?" (vs. the Angel de la Muerte). Once again the realist, Devon replies, "We moved. We went back to work. Real life happened." But Ellie won't let it go: "When do we get to take a break from real life? When do we get to be these people again?" Though Devon determines to grab some real food and watch their wedding video before recreating their wedding night, reality invades once more as he is called away for an emergency surgery…to save the life of Premier Goya of Costa Grava. However, the grateful premier comes knocking to invite them to a romantic gala at his consulate, where Ellie confides to Sarah that though the newlyweds have "hot and cold patches," moments return when it still "feels like it did in the beginning."

Pregnancy doesn't foster their romance either. "…Feeling a little 'over babied,'" Ellie tells Devon, " I'm not even four months pregnant and it's all we talk about" (vs. the Coup D'état). Not only is Devon now driving a minivan, but he can go an hour at a time addressing Ellie's stomach, not her. When opportunity comes knocking twice, the future parents gladly accept the offer of a babymoon vacation from the ever-grateful Premier Goya in Costa Grava. Taken with the romance of the palace gala, Ellie, licking her lips, displays a renewed "caliente" when flipping Devon's tie and asking him how he feels about "taking a tour of some of the darker corners" of the palace. And that's just where Chuck and Sarah walk in on them to observe a make-out session recalling the one on their first day at UCLA med school.

After Baby Clara arrives, the new parents gain even deeper insights into the reality of family life. Overwhelmed, Devon paces outside the apartment after completing a shift. Calling walking through the door "go time," he admits, "Trauma surgery's a cinch. It's coming home that's stressful" (vs. the A-Team). Indeed, Ellie, "stir crazy" from being home with the baby, "makes up for twelve hours of not talking to another adult in about twelve minutes," bombarding Awesome with statistical reports on Clara's sleep schedule and new vocal sounds. In a more relaxed moment, Ellie laments the fact that she's "just a stay-at-home mom," prompting her husband to rejoin, "You're not 'just' anything, Ellie." But as Devon himself confides a season later, "You know, when I first became a stay-at-home dad, I lost my identity." Claiming to have "adjusted 110%" to paternity leave and insisting, "I could do this forever," Devon later confesses "I was going nuts" (vs. the Business Trip). Ironically, watching Devon participate in his baby yoga sessions on her way to work causes Ellie to reconsider her own desires. Despite agreeing with Sarah that she's lucky Devon is willing to stay home with Clara, Ellie's expression belies her reply: "I'm a happy lady." By episode's end, Awesome reveals, "I was just putting up a front," and Ellie explains, "It was too soon for me to go back. Anyway, I missed her too much."

In addition to handling childhood baggage and adult challenges, Ellie, along with Devon, serves as an additional link to the real world for Sarah, given the agent's own missing links. Early in Season 1, Chuck and Sarah begin sharing cover dates with Devon and Ellie, a normal and successful couple that provides Sarah with a window to a 'real' relationship. As early as Episode 4 (vs. the Wookiee), the UCLA couple shows comfortable affection while playing the Newlywed Game, with Sarah quietly taking note, just as she does on their double date to sushi in Episode 8 (vs. the Truth). While listening to the story of how they met and Devon's sentimental comments about Ellie, particularly owning the color of her lucky sweater due to her eyes, Sarah indicates visible interest. Outside the restaurant, Sarah further studies Devon and Ellie kiss and snuggle, leading her to lean encouragingly into Chuck with a smirk and a coy glance up into his eyes before resting her own head on his chest.

As the series progresses, Sarah gains a first row seat to Ellie's difficult family dynamics, as well as her responses. Sarah looks on silently in Season 2 at the caterer's tasting while Devon's parents suffocate Ellie…and Ellie draws a line. In Season 3, during a season of distance between Chuck and Sarah, Sarah listens attentively to Ellie's admission of dry spells in marriage during which they "put passion on hold" before assuring her, "…Being here in a place like this…brings it all back" (vs. the Coup D'état). In Season 4 (vs. the First Fight), Sarah observes perhaps Ellie's most vulnerable moment: the reunion with her estranged mother, a dynamic that Sarah understands only too well. Not coincidentally, Sarah is repeatedly placed between Ellie and her mother in the frame, suggesting Sarah is caught between Mary's position, given her need to leave the baby she saved from Ryker to her mother, and Ellie's position as the abandoned child given the track record of Sarah's father.

These windows into the life of a mature, successful woman in the real world not only guide Sarah but enable her to feel safe in turning to Ellie in times of her own need. During her engagement to Chuck, Sarah admits her general sense of "terror" to Ellie, and in particular her angst over Chuck's impulse to invite the C.A.T. team to the engagement party (vs. the CAT Squad). Ellie simply listens and sympathizes before ending the conversation with an invitation: "Sarah, if you ever need to talk about complicated family situations, wedding stuff, anything, you can come to me." With sincerity, Sarah smiles, admitting, "It does feel good to talk about it." Ellie later approaches Chuck to provide some insight on seeing life through the windows of others, not just his own, and leaves him with a new concept: "…Sometimes the best thing you can do is take a step back… You don't have to fix everything." At the engagement party, Ellie also anticipates Sarah's melancholy over her "complicated" family. Keeping an appropriate distance, Ellie offers to talk about it with Sarah later if she desires, noting, "We're practically family, right?...More importantly, we're friends." With this encouragement, Sarah musters the courage to ask Ellie to become her maid of honor. Careful to temper her excitement, Ellie dignifies the request with a heart-felt and tearful hug that puts her future sister-in-law at ease, another family link forged.

Not surprisingly, Sarah turns to Ellie for help in navigating through her wedding plans, too. In fact, it is Ellie's input about finding one thing that will spark an interest in the others that a skeptical Sarah ultimately discovers to be true when Ellie suggests focusing on the dress. From there, it is all downhill. Sarah's observance of Ellie's change in priorities upon becoming a mother likely affects Sarah's own shift in Season 5 as well. Not only does she warm up to the idea of starting a family with Chuck, from which she earlier distanced herself, but eventually presents a plan to transition out of the traditional spy business to a safer, more family-friendly version of Carmichael Industries.

At series' end, Ellie's superior analytic skills emerge as the final facet of her evolving character. The discovery of her father's computer spurs Ellie to pursue the mission of deciphering its contents, linking her to the larger purpose she has missed as a stay-at-home mom. Though Chuck initially succeeds in separating Ellie from the computer, Director Bentley secretly returns it to her after the failed A-Team Intersect Project so she can continue her father's work in neurobiology. And when Chuck discovers Bentley's action and moves to sideline Ellie once again, Bentley leaves him with a word of advice before her reassignment: "You know, your sister is incredibly smart. If anyone can figure out the Intersect, it's her. You may want to reconsider keeping her away from her path" (vs. the Muuurder).

Conflicted, Chuck still opts to protect Ellie by asking Devon to erase the computer's hard drive. But when Devon lies to Chuck about doing so, Ellie continues to work in secret. After the computer scans her face as she sleeps one night, Ellie awakes to find additional files pertaining to a project known as the Intersect and a mysterious Agent X. Invigorated, Ellie tells Devon, "I figured out a cycloramic complexity that ran through all the conditionals in my dad's research," to explain how she ended up with the photo of Agent X's childhood home (vs. Agent X). And after Chuck salvages the hard drive damaged on the bachelor party trip to find the photo and redacted files, the Castle crew ultimately succeeds in identifying Volkoff as Agent X, though Casey convinces them it must remain a secret for everyone's safety. At that point Ellie suggests the mission is a private one left by their father for his children to work together not merely to find Agent X but also fix him. Before they get the chance, though, Decker transforms Volkoff back into Hartley with his own pair of Intersect glasses.

However, Ellie continues to work on the neurobiological front to help others restore missing mental and emotional links. A concerned Sarah seeks Ellie out to ask about Morgan's abnormal behavior and amnesia resulting from his downloading of the Intersect (vs. the Frosted Tips). After pointing out the likelihood that a modified version of her dad's program is responsible, Ellie offers insight on how to help Morgan recall his real identity: "I've had temporal lobe patients who have responded to stories about who they were before the injury. It doesn't return them to normal, but….It gives them a glimpse of who they used to be." Using Ellie's suggestion, Chuck succeeds in helping Morgan remember his real identity on the helipad by recalling a junior high incident Chuck helped him through, saving their friendship. Later, Ellie conceives of using the Intersect glasses to help Sarah regain her memories at the end of Season 5 by loading them with images from her past. Though convinced it will work, Ellie is never given the chance, since Chuck must use the last upload to save a concert hall full of people.

The Ellie that leaves with Devon for Chicago as the curtain falls on "Chuck" has evolved from the big sister throwing Chuck's birthday party in the pilot, passing through many phases of intermediary development. Now a married woman with a child, she has also healed the gaps in her parental relationships while preserving a relationship with her brother and forging one with her sister-in-law. In the end, Ellie successfully links herself to others and restores vital links missing for years, but she is still far too young to be called anyone's fossil.

CHAPTER **18:**

Raw Oysters

Casey's internal growth (see Chapter 15: Wall Comes Tumbling Down) brings with it a bonus in Season 5: an openness to pursuing a long-term relationship with a woman besides his daughter, spy competitor Gertrude Verbanski. In doing so, however, Casey is challenged with further improving his still-challenged communication skills. While the collapsing wall metaphor still generally applies to Casey within the context of this new relationship, an additional set of images is overlaid to specifically figure Casey's unorthodox romance with Verbanski.

The "point of conception" for Casey's relationship with Gertrude occurs during an evening "recon" mission, with Sarah quarterbacking from the van (vs. the Frosted Tips). During the staged 'chance' intercept on a city sidewalk, the viewer pointedly discovers Verbanski's favorite restaurant is a raw oyster bar called Cerulean, where she craves Blue Point oysters. Casey enthusiastically agrees with her culinary taste, especially when they are glazed with savory mignonette sauce. Gertrude, mugging her lower lip with her upper, admits she could "go for some right now," and it doesn't seem like she only has dinner on her mind. As Sarah notes through Casey's earpiece, "The target is yours! Ask her out." But unable to find the words after a couple of silent moments, the NSA colonel instead offers only a goodbye handshake and pat on her shoulder. Though Casey fails to capitalize on Gertrude's overture, the metaphorical framework is set for a problematic relationship between two emotionally isolated souls struggling with communication skills (i.e. proverbial oysters) that enjoy their love-making raw and peppery, if not in fact spicy.

The sexual portion of this dynamic becomes clear even before Casey and Gertrude actually start dating. While racing over to save Chuck and the Morgansect from the ill-advised raid on Sneijder's office (vs. the Bearded Bandit), Casey reveals to Sarah that he shared an "incredible" romp with Verbanski in his past….after she had just tried to kill him no less. Sarah almost swerves out of her lane. The first private moment the two oysters share after the 'chance' intercept, when Gertrude discovers Casey raiding her office to retrieve the flash drive Morgan stole from Castle, reinforces this spicy dynamic (vs. the Frosted Tips). Saturated with sensuality, the scene presents the two spies' struggle to subdue one another and ends with Gertrude asking, "Enough foreplay?" However, Casey leaves her cuffed to the furniture, longing for more. By episode's conclusion, Casey is running through rooftop flames to save Gertrude from an exploding chopper. His reward? A make-out session on the roof, followed by a date at the shooting range.

However, Casey's subsequent killing of the Viper and her assassin team complicates their blossoming sexcapade. Arrested by Decker for murder, Casey is remanded to federal prison, but that obstacle doesn't keep Gertrude from linking up with her man. Just as two inmates converge on Chuck with evil intent, Gertrude, in guard uniform, grabs him from behind and throws him into a cleaning closet for a "conjugal visit" (vs. the Hack Off). Before proceeding with that visit, Gertrude apologizes if she was too physical, but Casey won't hear of it, claiming, "I actually enjoyed it." Similarly, when they travel to Miami for an arms deal with Falcone, Gertrude suggests they "work up an appetite" before dinner by pulling him into the bedroom by his bathrobe belt (vs. the Kept Man). Sarah, fearing the worst in Gertrude's sudden disappearance, enters the Presidential Suite with gun drawn only to gag when observing Verbanski spank a "naughty colonel." When Chuck arrives outside the door, noticing her comic horror, he asks Sarah what is wrong. She can only reply, "Everything. It's all wrong."

Of course, Gertrude and Casey's relationship grows beyond sheer sensual magnetism, and as it does, the focus shifts to their limited abilities, as metaphorical oysters, in terms of open communication and emotional engagement. While leaving that conjugal visit, Gertrude grants Casey's wish to assist Carmichael Industries, which is "a man down," until he returns (vs. the Hack Off). That translates into Verbanski joining the Castle Couple on the mission to the nudist colony to find the Omen virus-maker Colin Davis. After they return with Davis in tow, Sarah, noticing Gertrude "on edge," reaches out, offering, "We can talk about it if you want." Seemingly speaking of herself in the plural, Verbanski bluntly informs Sarah, "We don't talk." While she speaks, however, Gertrude notably pours herself a glass of water from a tall, transparent pitcher, signifying change is on the horizon. But not just yet. When Sarah pursues the topic, specifically asking if her mood is related to Casey, all she receives in return is a decidedly Casey-esque grunt. Before Gertrude leaves in a huff, throwing an insult like a grenade on her way, Sarah manages to slip in, "You know, you can still have feelings for somebody and still be a good spy."

At first, Sarah's words seem to have no effect. But their conversation continues soon thereafter, taking an ironic turn while they infiltrate The Collective compound together during the Hack-Off. After Sarah asks a clearly mission-oriented question, Gertrude, her mind obviously elsewhere, suddenly unfastens her thoughts: "Fine! I love Casey. Just stop grilling me!" As her shell continues to open, without too much prying, Gertrude admits she's been "a wreck" since Casey's jailing and didn't realize she had "such strong feelings for him." She even goes so far as to confess she is "petrified it might actually turn into something," though, God forbid, not kids or quitting the spy life. Chuck's unlikely protégé, ready to help, counsels, "Relationships are all about communication, so big life changes don't spring up on you like that."

In a limited fashion, Casey and Gertrude start down the road of more transparent communication soon thereafter. When Gertrude realizes that Chuck has become the fall guy in Decker's plot to obtain the Omen virus and Casey will rot in prison forever, she leaves Decker with a grenade in his pocket (vs. the Hack-Off). But before she leaves town for things to blow over, she makes one last visit to break Casey out and openly laments, "We could have been something." Matching her, Casey openly disagrees: "We still can." Alas, Casey is correct: after Beckman puts "a lid" on the Decker incident, a future awaits them, but it is not exactly the one Casey envisioned.

Verbanski returns to surprise Casey at his apartment and stay the night, but the next turn in their relationship shows they both still have room for growth. In the morning, Gertrude presents her favorite Blue Point with a pair of presents, the first a notably cerulean Kashmir sweater (vs. the Kept Man). In contrast to Casey's pointed concerns over its "soft" texture and flammability, Gertrude's gift indicates the further softening of her emotional shell. The second gift? A vacation to Miami at the Maya. Casey, not as thrilled with this one, declines a bit gruffly, citing work obligations. Not coincidentally, Casey struggles with wearing the supple, blue garment, irritably fingering the collar while receiving Chuck's memo on the new C.A.R.E. mission statement (Clandestine Agents Relating Emotionally) of Carmichael Industries. Of course Casey pans the equally soft new company philosophy and bristles at Chuck's calling Gertrude his "girlfriend," denying it. Casey's inner turmoil surrounding these emotional infringements is further highlighted in a seemingly innocuous comment made by Jeffster. While monitoring Buy More surveillance footage, they notice Casey wearing the sweater, forcing them to question, "Who are you, John Casey?" Ultimately, the sweater will find its way into the trash when Casey becomes overwhelmed by the dynamics of the relationship.

Undeterred by Casey's response to the South Beach vacation, Gertrude finds another way to have her man served on the half shell. Within hours of Chuck's significant addition of the C.A.R.E. slogan to the company website, Gertrude, furthering her contrast with Casey, hires Carmichael Industries for the Falcone arms mission in Miami, citing the "personal service" it offers. When not tackling hotel employees into the pool, Casey balks at wearing the Speedo Gertrude purchases for him. And while arguing with Sarah over whether or not he is going to put it on in the changing cabana, he complains, "...She doesn't listen to what I'm tryin' to tell her." Matters don't improve over dinner. Casey balks at going to an unsecure location to complete the arms deal, causing Gertrude to reply, "John, I want those guns, and when I want something--." The end of the sentence is a grip of his upper thigh under the table before toasting, "...Here's to playing harder." Casey flees for the bar, where he's greeted as Mr. Verbanski.

Chuck follows, only to find Casey clamming up again. When asked if he cares for advice, Casey spews, "Use the word 'care' again, I'm going to take this glass, shove it down your throat, and punch you in the stomach until it shatters." But then the colonel unhinges his shell just a tad. "She doesn't want a relationship; she wants a lackey, a lapdog...a beefcake." Chuck responds with a brief lecture on semiotics. "What is Verbanski really trying to tell you?...Tough women like Gertrude and Sarah are constantly giving out these signals that you need to be sensitive to. ...You need to learn how to listen with your heart." Casey returns to the table with Chuck, but, as with Sarah's conversation with Gertrude earlier, it remains immediately unclear whether Chuck's Dutch uncle act has any effect.

Initially, the answer appears to be no. When Gertrude has her own personnel bail them out on the drop, Casey thinks he and Carmichael Industries have been played and wants out, even though Verbanski claims this is the first part of a larger deal and she needs him for what is left. And when Gertrude is taken hostage on that ensuing mission, he sees it as only another manipulative ruse. Awakened by a phone call from Pedro St. Germaine, her captor in the Everglades, Casey is eventually slapped into reality. That is, he hears St. Germaine slapping Gertrude over the line followed by her muffled shouting that ends with "Casey, I can take care of myself!" The deal? "$10,000,000 by tonight or she dies."

Suddenly mobilized, Casey races to Florida, where he briefs Chuck and Sarah on the mission, including a peculiar code word. While negotiating with St. Germaine at gunpoint, Casey, buying time, has to improvise on his code phrase "Care" when no response is forthcoming. Ultimately, his impromptu speech turns into a heart-felt confession mirroring Chuck's advice at the bar: "I've been working so hard on my spy sense….What I should have been working on is this" (gesturing to his heart). Urged to stop by Gertrude, he continues. "No, I can't, Gertrude, because I love you…And I need you to know how much I care…I care a lot!" Overhearing the speech, Chuck, a proud sensei, congratulates Casey on "opening up your heart like that" even in the midst of their escape attempt.

As the Verbanski arc comes to a close, so do the former oysters' emotional and verbal issues. Gertrude enters Castle with a garment bag that initially gives Casey pause. But after she assures him, he unzips the bag to find a flak jacket emblazoned "Colonel John Casey," followed beneath by "Love, Gertrude." She proceeds to apologize for her earlier 'kept man' approach, explaining, "It was my misguided way of saying….I want to be close to you." Though less elegant, Casey follows suit: "Thanks….I feel the same." And though Casey declines Gertrude's offer to join her on a mission, due to the other woman in his life, the road is open to rejoin Gertrude at series' end, their trials having produced the lustrous gem of openness and honesty.

CHAPTER 19:

Morgan Rising

You have reached your mid-twenties. Yet, you have to be instructed to leave your best friend's house in the late hours of the evening. So you shuffle out the door for the ride home…on your bike. When you arrive, you walk past the computer you fried with a porn virus, just like the one at work. While your best friend is on a date, you have nothing better to do, so you call him to ask how the date is going. From your friend's bedroom. Lying on your friend's bed. And when your best friend scores another hot dinner date at his house, you show up unannounced to join them, because you took him literally when he left work, saying, "See you later."

Welcome to the Season 1 reality of Morgan Grimes, who is held in such low regard that even the Buy Morons claim the local Sbarro has named a "Loser" pizza after him: "no sauce, no topping, nothing but pure cheese" (vs. the Imported Hard Salami). Though Morgan remains in a state of arrested development for roughly half of the series, he does eventually succeed in maturing both personally and professionally to assume a responsible and productive role in society. No one summarizes this dramatic transformation better than the incredulous Mr. Grimes himself when he muses to his erstwhile roommate, Casey, "Just think. In five years I went from pip-squeaky side-kick to this" (vs. Sarah).

Morgan's path from pathetical to respectable perhaps best illustrates itself in the upward progression of his romantic relationships, which coincides with his professional advancement. At the outset, the hapless Buy More green shirt continues to suffer from an infatuation with his best friend's sister, Ellie. The fact that she lives with a former Abercrombie and Fitch model boasting an M.D. doesn't seem to deter Morgan, nor does body language that oozes with repulsion, as Ellie does when she leans as far away as possible when he sits down next to her on the fountain in the pilot. Words have little effect either. After advising Ellie she can tell him her deepest, darkest secrets, she responds, "Here's one: I loathe you" (vs. the Helicopter). No matter. Morgan keeps her on a pedestal and—irony of ironies--even has the opportunity to emotionally bond when both are distraught over Chuck's seeming preoccupation with Sarah (vs. the Sizzling Shrimp). Later, a drunk Ellie perceives Devon to have only "one foot in" their relationship (vs. the Undercover Lover). In the aftermath of the latter, Ellie actually hugs Morgan with friendly relief upon discovering that he did not take advantage of her even though they awake in the same bed. Accordingly, Morgan proceeds to reassure Ellie that she is like a sister to him….just one that he wants to have sex with. Forgetting Ellie takes a while.

Morgan initially finds distraction in a thoroughly adolescent relationship with Anna. Unfazed by Morgan's penchant for using camcorders to broadcast women's thong underwear storewide, which even Chuck chastises as "13-year-old" behavior, or Morgan's last place standing in store sales competitions, Anna finds herself drawn to Morgan's gaming skills. Their coupling begins appropriately enough on the couch in the Buy More video room during a session of "Call of Duty" (vs. the Imported Hard Salami). When Anna confides he's one of the best players at the store, Morgan dubiously interprets her attention as an opportunity to "jam his tongue down [her] throat." Despite his ensuing rejection, leaving him sprawled on the floor, Morgan still tries to salvage a shred of self-respect by clarifying exactly where he stands in the Buy More pecking order, asking, "But you'd take me over Lester, right?"

Documentaries on lone wolves can prove an intoxicating aphrodisiac, however. Succumbing to Morgan's animal magnetism, Anna soon slides back on to the video room couch to hear him laud the wisdom of the predators on the screen, which jump from mate to mate. Anna sagely counters, "Maybe. But lone wolves are also lonely." The peck she leaves on Morgan's cheek not only indicates that he does in fact rank above Lester but also serves as the green light to a relationship that sets new standards for "inappropriately short skirts" and PDA, even for the Buy More (vs. the Crown Vic). The quality of their relationship is placed on further display when Anna spends an evening as the hostile Thanksgiving guest of Ellie Bartowski, who she perceives as Morgan's 'ex,' and unilaterally competes with her hostess for Morgan's culinary affection (vs. the Nemesis).

Eventually, Morgan's deadbeat ways wear thin even on Anna, who, "sick of hooking up only at work," puts her heel down (vs. the DeLorean). Morgan at first argues there is nowhere else to go: "My mother's always home; you have three roommates." But when Anna insists they're ready to take the next step and move in together, he switches tactics, insisting they are "living the dream" in a video room featuring "72-inch plasma, super-comfy couches, and all the free coffee we can drink." With Anna unconvinced, Morgan accepts a move-in check from Awesome with his congratulations: "Welcome to adulthood, Morgan. We've been waiting for you." However, Morgan delays his arrival a tad longer when he opts for a beat-up DeLorean instead. Even when presented with a second chance after the 'stolen' car is impounded, Morgan resists moving in with a ridiculously detailed "Morgannuptial" that, to his disappointment, Anna will still gladly sign (vs. the Lethal Weapon). Upon getting wind of Morgan's "testing" of Anna, Chuck delicately suggests to him, "You are lucky to have a girl in your life who loves you..for you..even though you are, in fact..you." With a single, pronounced nod of the head, Morgan concedes, "Fair."

Season 2 ends with Morgan chasing his dream in Hawaii with Anna, but Season 3 begins with his return from a nightmare after Anna runs off with the prep chef. By the time she visits Burbank late in Season 3 (vs. the Tooth), though, Anna finds Assistant Manager Grimes a new man. Jeffster informs the skeptical "ex" that "Morgan is in a very bad place…He's focused, responsible, driven." But when Morgan appears in a tux for a concert mission with Chuck and gives Anna less than half the time of day, he leaves her a believer, gasping, "Wow!" Morgan gives her even less attention on her next visit, and after he declines the gadgets from his past she brings on a final trip, she makes a pass at him, explaining, "You know what they say about not knowing you want something until you can't have it?…You've changed, Morgan. I want you back." Morgan pauses a moment before soberly replying, "If it took me running from you to realize I'm something you want then I don't think you're really the person that I want. So, you're right. I have changed." And good thing, too. In two episodes, Alex will walk into the Buy More…and his life.

Morgan's interaction with Carina, which bookends his relationship with Anna, tells a similar tale. The Season 1 installment of the unlikely couple returns Morgan to his most pitiful era. Aware he is a "third wheel" once Chuck starts dating Sarah, he pleads with Chuck to let him be a "fourth wheel, for once" on a double date (vs. the Wookiee). Used by Sarah merely to keep the conniving Carina away from Chuck, Morgan drools over the sexy spy with a middle school come-on: "Were you always this hot, or did you recently find your hotness?" Ultimately, "Martin" is also used by Carina, who can't even remember his name, to dump her diamond during a staged kiss before she in turn dumps him and his flowers. And all just when Morgan is on the cusp of a noble beau geste: offering to "treat" her to coffee, one for each! The rejection ends up sending him on a grape soda bender.

Things improve considerably on the second go round with Carina in Season 3 after Morgan, still licking his wounds from his Hawaiian venture, finds his spine (vs. the Three Words). Though Carina walks right past Morgan at the Buy More to retrieve Chuck for a briefing in Castle, she eventually returns to leave him a briefcase for Chuck. Later that evening, she ends up arriving at "Martin's" apartment during a raging party with an entourage of thugs to wait for Chuck in the "VIP lounge," though Morgan doesn't realize she is at gunpoint. Embarrassed by the snubs, Morgan finally bursts, "…My name is not Martin! It's Morgan! …Memorize it!" before continuing, "…Just because you're a beautiful woman that I would give a non-vital organ to make love to, doesn't give you the right to show up with this crowd and humiliate me in front of my friends!" But when things get dicey beyond Morgan's frame of reference, Carina suggests that he leave, only for Morgan to turn the tables: "My house, my party. I think you need to leave….[There are] 730 words in the Japanese language for the word yes; no word for 'no.' But if there was a Japanese word for 'no,' I'd be saying it right now." Next morning, thanks to some heroics by the Castle team, Morgan finds himself waking up in bed with Carina, who explains, "No one's ever said 'no' to me before. It's sexy." To his delight, she adds, "…I've had better…but not many."

By Sarah's engagement party in Season 4 (vs. the CAT Squad), Carina, like Anna before her, ironically pursues the Buy More's new Alex-struck manager, who also just happens to be moonlighting as a CIA operative. No sooner has she descended from the helicopter into the courtyard than she circles Morgan, observing, "Something's different about you." And after he wakes up next morning stunned to find Carina clothed only in a sheet, he hears her confirm her initial assessment:

"Something is different about you. The confidence. The straight spine. It can't be true, but, you're behaving like you're having regular sexual intercourse."

She soon discovers just how correct her assessment is. Refusing to obey her command to "get back in this bed," Morgan confronts Carina over ignoring his emails, snail mail and texts before informing her, "I'm off the market. OK? So, I would like you to leave." When even standing stark naked in front of Morgan doesn't budge him, it leaves Carina only with thoughts of sabotage. After Morgan, who is assigned to "babysit" the injured Carina at Castle, resists her further overtures, she resorts to planting lipstick on his shirt collar, before finally apologizing to Alex when she sees them reconcile at the party. Who'd have thunk?

The relatively mature relationship Morgan and Alex share bears little resemblance to those that precede it. The sensitive and confident Buy More manager who saves Alex from Jeffster when she arrives with Casey's locker key at the end of Season 3 is a dramatic upgrade from the green-shirted dead beat of Seasons 1 and 2. However, given the intimidating presence of Alex's father, their romantic link builds slowly in Season 4, when even acknowledging the exchange of pot roast recipes poses its risks (vs. the Coup D'état). Impatient, Alex speeds things up with a successful pass on Morgan in the manager's office before explaining, "I know you're freaked out about my dad, but I want to do this. Do you?" When Morgan responds with ramblings about Dr. Fred's steps, a disenchanted Alex backs away before turning to make her way to the door. But she doesn't reach it. Unable to watch her leave, Morgan grabs Alex by the arm and pulls her back into his embrace, resigning himself, "Aw, screw it!"

Still, the waters remain troubled when Morgan next drags his feet on informing Casey of their dating, so much so that Alex again shows signs of cold feet at his cowardice (vs. the Couch Lock). It gets more "complicated" when Morgan has to leave Alex not only with the impression that playing Halo takes priority over their relationship but that he is breaking up with her to keep her out of the path of a dangerous thug looking for Casey in the courtyard. Unwilling to lose her, Morgan hits two birds with one stone by notifying Casey of their romance while couch-locked: not only is the anticipated bodily damage inflicted upon Morgan minimized, but he succeeds in rapidly expediting Casey's recovery from the paralysis in time to save the mission. But is there still a romance to save? Just when it appears that Fate has denied him, Alex arrives unexpectedly at his party with an equally unexpected, if not entirely accurate, revelation. Informing Morgan that Casey has told her the whole story, Alex is impressed with how Morgan, after first breaking up with her at her father's insistence, stood up to him to change his mind. "Maybe I was wrong about you," she concludes. "You are brave."

As their relationship grows, new depths appear in Morgan's character, including a change in his priorities. Chuck's eyebrows raise when he observes his roommate display more concern with Alex than the pizza and orange juice stains she threatens to leave on the "previously unworn original issue Zemeckis-authenticated Back to the Future t-shirt" she borrows after spending the night (vs. the Gobbler). When Chuck advises there is still time to save the shirt, Morgan replies, "It's cool," and notes Alex looks cute in it. The change, though, scares Morgan, who asks, "What the hell's wrong with me?" Wearing a paternal smile, Chuck replies, "Nothing's wrong with you, my friend. But I have news for you, Morgan. I think you're in love." But he's not yet ready to tell her.

Another dimension reveals itself when Morgan finds the capacity to comfort Alex in her time of deepest grief. Joining Alex at Casey's hospital bedside after Sarah sends him through a window to a multi-story plunge, Morgan quietly assures Alex her father is going to be OK, adding, "And he loves you, too. Trust me. More than you know." The next day, the encouragement persists with an observation: "He's the strongest man I've ever met, OK? He'll pull through" (vs. the Push Mix).

But Carina's return for Sarah's engagement party places Morgan in altogether new territory. Unfamiliar with how to communicate Carina's unsought and unwelcome advances, especially given his past tryst with the sultry spy, Morgan allows a gap of insecurity to form between Alex and him. Threatened and confused by the "leggy girls" and "half-truths" of the spy world Morgan inhabits, Alex, not feeling "special," pulls back. And even though she stops shy of accusing Morgan of unfaithfulness, she informs him, "We're done." A stricken Morgan stops Alex as she walks away with more words of assurance: "I want you to know something: nothing happened, because nothing means more to me than this relationship. I'd never do anything to threaten that, ever." Finally, he finds the words he lacked before, confessing, "I love you....I love you....I'm in love with you." By the time Carina walks up to apologize, it already doesn't matter. Cutting her off while hardly taking her eyes off Morgan, Alex tells her, "It's OK: he loves me."

Morgan and Alex do not immediately live happily ever after. Indeed, the Morgansect arc presents a significant setback that Morgan punctuates with an exclamation mark when he breaks up with Alex by text message. As matters play out, Morgan's victimization due to the tainted Intersect program intended for Chuck becomes evident. Regardless, the pain caused by the revelation of "his inner jerk" throbs for Alex much longer than the punch to the gut that her father gives Morgan after the Intersect is removed (vs. the Business Trip). Morgan's attempt to win her back gets off to a rocky start at the Buy More when he tries to explain he had a supercomputer in his head "melting" his brain and claims he is being hunted by an "elusive assassin." A wide-eyed Alex initially considers Morgan "legitimately insane," but his credibility rises instantly when he points out the pistol-wielding Viper stalking the store before telling Alex he loves her and depositing her safely in a closet.

The reconciliation process picks up steam with the revelation of his P.A.N.T.S. box, containing "Private Artifacts Never To Share" (vs. the Curse). Given Morgan's "most sacred possessions" for safe-keeping, Alex opens the box to discover a photo of them together prominently displayed beneath her college graduation announcement. Moved but not yet convinced, Alex is encouraged by others to take a second look. After a game night in Castle (vs. the Baby), Awesome assures her, "Trust me, he loves you." Then even Casey gives her the green light: "You know that Grimes kid? He's not that bad. You should maybe give him another chance." Ironically, the clincher comes while watching Morgan play with a responsive Molly when Emma brings her to the apartment for safe-keeping. Visibly impressed, Alex follows Morgan into a corner, where she lets her kiss do most of the talking. In the end, the game night advice to Morgan from Ellie, who formerly loathed him, not only proves prophetic, but puts the distance Morgan has journeyed into distinct perspective: "Stop trying to force it. You are a catch. She's gonna realize that soon enough."

Morgan's espionage career shows an ascendant pattern similar to his romantic relationships. In the early days after his integration into Project Bartowski, Morgan's performance can be classified as categorically inept. Hungry for affirmation, Morgan displays himself as "desperate, stupid, or just plain willing to do anything...."

(vs. the Tic Tac), a fact that a rogue Casey plays to his advantage when getting a suspicious-looking Morgan to ape the actions of a real spy and retrieve the Laudanol from the Buy More. Pointedly, the pill is placed in a "Planet of the Apes" DVD, a movie Morgan claims to hate, and a video screen in the next aisle features a screaming ape pounding its chest and looking in Morgan's direction. When confronted by Chuck, a dejected Morgan finally admits, "This is my first mission, Chuck, and I don't want to screw it up." But Chuck knows exactly how to appeal to the wannabe spy: in exchange for the DVD he promises to answer any questions Morgan has about his real missions "in sordid detail." The DVD is suddenly his for the taking.

Morgan proceeds to approach his espionage career like an amateur with a romanticized and overconfident perspective. Impatient for action, he tells Casey, "This whole G-man gig is starting to become a real snore, you know? When do we get to put some hurt on some terrorists?" To underscore his readiness, he dubiously engages in a little faux kung-fu (vs. the Role Models). "Whatever it is you think you know about being a spy, you're wrong," Casey replies, unimpressed, bluntly adding, "You're a child. You're a liability to the team, and you're not doing anything until you're properly trained. Understood?"

Training begins immediately on the three key elements: subversion, stealth, and strength. Morgan, thinking he's already mastered the first two, soon receives a reality check. Tasked with obtaining a "hottie's" phone number, he returns with a business card scrawled, "You disgust me!" Likewise, Morgan fails bagging Big Mike's card key. Still, Morgan thinks passing his shooting range test will be "no problem;" he plays a lot of first-person shooting games, after all. After assuring himself, "Just like 'Call of Duty,'" the pistol leaps out of his hand on first pull of the trigger. Even though Morgan acknowledges he "failed every test," Casey piles on: "With flying colors. You have got to be hands down, bar none, the worst candidate I've ever trained…"

Like his progressive success with the ladies, the former ape of a spy increasingly finds ways to meaningfully serve his country, though the evolutionary process isn't always pretty. Even as Morgan's missions vary in degrees of success and occasionally betray a lingering ineptitude, one undeniably admirable trait emerges: courage. When Casey and he are pinned down in the Echo Park courtyard by a full-grown Bengal tiger, Morgan decides to use his legs to lure the predator into Awesome and Ellie's apartment (vs. the Role Models). The feat earns him Casey's back-handed praise: "…You've got one thing going for you: you got balls….How many Marines you know would go up against a Bengal tiger unarmed? You've got to be a complete idiot." Morgan's heroic gesture at the Buy More, when he tries to save Casey from Volkoff's minions, yields less success (vs. the Leftovers). Hidden in a closet, Morgan courageously concocts a potentially suicidal plan: to come out with his hands behind his head and a pistol taped to his back. But when the moment comes to seize the weapon and blow the baddies away--while yelling "Yippee Ki Yay!" no less--he can't reach it even after several tries. Good thing Volkoff had already called his team off.

In perhaps Morgan's most ironic turn, the paper-shredding General Beckman, moments from her arrest by a Ring-controlled CIA, tells him, "As much as it pains me to admit this, you are our only hope" (vs. the Living Dead). Though displaying the intestinal fortitude to trail Shaw's armored car holding his Castle colleagues, he doesn't actually have a plan when Shaw prepares to execute his prisoners. Thankfully sheer luck smiles upon him when Awesome and he accidentally push the right buttons in Casey's Crown Vic, enabling Team Bartowski to live another day. And when Morgan is later tied up back at the Buy More, he manages not only to get to his phone but call Casey for help. With Casey too far away, only one option remains: break his thumbs to escape and clear the Buy More before Shaw's bomb explodes. Incredibly, Morgan 2.0 follows through…only to find the alarm activated in a Pineapple plot by Big Mike and Jeffster just before Morgan reaches the box. Of course, the thumb-swaddled hero subsequently finds a way to diminish his exploit by dropping the detonator when he finds it, eviscerating the Buy More.

Believe it or not, Morgan is also credited with performing "the single bravest thing" Chuck has ever seen (vs. the Couch Lock). While in Iran with Casey to save Chuck and Sarah, Morgan is tasked with pushing a button on a control panel to cut the lights in the bunker. When the signal is given, Morgan does as he is told, but bad luck intervenes and shorted circuitry begins to fill the bunker with water. More button pushing leads to electrical shorting and hanging live wires. Unilaterally surrendering despite Casey's bluster about a squad poised outside, Morgan joins his captive mates inside looking for redemption. Seizing the chance, he jumps into the rising water with the live wire, effectively allowing 10,000 volts to jolt his body and send him into cardiac arrest. The bad guys don't fare well either. Perhaps a bit jealous, Casey proves less impressed than Chuck after he revives, noting Morgan was only dead for three seconds.

Not all of Morgan's espionage career yields mixed results, however. His exploits as the Intersect notwithstanding, Code Name Cobra does attain multiple moments of success without asterisks. The first, occurring in Season 3, foreshadows Morgan's promise. With Chuck and Sarah off-grid, Beckman tasks Casey to use Morgan to find them (vs. the Honeymooners). In a series of brilliant conclusions, Morgan, who calls himself "the Intersect of Chuck," triangulates Chuck's need for a filled prescription, the nearest train station, and his penchant for CD Comics to locate Chuck standing next to a magazine rack en route to Zurich within minutes. Impressed, Casey feels obliged to inform Beckman of his "resourceful" partner at the mission's conclusion. Similarly, Morgan provides a ray of hope in the search for Chuck by turning up a key link to The Belgian after a desperate Sarah has reached a dead end (vs. Phase Three). Showing her a photo obtained from the Swiss field office, Morgan identifies Anand Chanarong, a Thai diplomat known for handling The Belgian's "dirty work" and further notes that he happens to be in Los Angeles at the Thai embassy. Morgan has barely completed his briefing before Sarah exits the room pursuing the lead that ends with finding Chuck.

Morgan also contributes significantly by smoothing over relationships in a manner that keeps missions on track instead of derailing. Concerned over Sarah going "Kill Bill" with the Thai diplomat during his interrogation, Morgan informs Casey so as to avoid "an international incident" (vs. Phase Three). And when things subsequently get heated between Casey and Sarah, Morgan literally wedges his way between them long enough to let cooler minds prevail. Morgan also salvages the interrogation of his old acquaintance Mary Bartowski when she stonewalls Casey and Sarah as to Chuck's whereabouts (vs. the First Fight). Instructed by Casey to stay behind the one-way window looking into the detention room, he hears Casey ignore Mary's demand to see Ellie followed by Mary's claim that "the only one I know I can trust is my son." While Sarah holds Casey back, Morgan ignores his directive, stepping in to the interrogation and engaging the stunned woman, who hasn't seen her son's best friend since he was nine years old. Morgan helps Mary recover from their unlikely reunion—and reset emotionally--by cheerfully reflecting on her Rice Krispy treats of old. But then he turns serious, confessing that

Chuck's disappearance is "a little bit my fault" and promising that she will get to see Ellie if she tells them where he is. Placing his unique credibility with her on the line, he quietly assures her, "You can trust me, Mrs. B." She deals.

Morgan has shining moments in the field, too. When the Castle crew raids the Thai jungle for the Belgian, Morgan serves ably as the magnet, facing a large force of weapon-wielding guards while posing as a lost backpacker, allowing Sarah and Casey to gain access to the compound with minimal resistance (vs. Phase Three). Alternatively, he shows uncanny agility and nimbleness when avoiding the laser beams protecting the Hydra network control center on the Countessa, gaining the team access to it (vs. the Push Mix). He manages to lose most of his clothes, but all his vital organs and limbs remain intact. And when called on to pose as an Italian arms dealer in Moscow at the bidding summit for The Norseman arranged by Vivian Volkoff, Morgan shows the sense and nerve to play dead long after the device is used (vs. the Last Details). Even the MI6 agent, the only other "bidder" to live through the ordeal, falls prey to Riley's ruse to detect survivors while Morgan remains silent and immobile. Even then, Morgan maintains uncanny composure when Casey must subsequently snipe the remaining Volkoff minions from a rooftop across the street using Morgan's video feed while the windows are blinded.

Morgan achieves perhaps his most poignant accomplishment in both romance and espionage in a moment that merges the two worlds. In the series finale, Morgan sits with Chuck, distraught over his lost love with Sarah, on the edge of the fountain with one last piece of detective work to offer: finding Sarah. With Chuck lamenting, "Morgan, she could be anywhere," Morgan confidently replies, "…You know where she is. You once told me to listen to our hearts, because our brains always screw us up." Chuck retreats, claiming, "I was in love then." But Morgan covers his flank: "You're still in love. I want you to imagine something for me, OK? Where is she? Right now. Don't think; use your heart. Where is she?" Just as Morgan gave Sarah the lead to find Chuck in her darkest hour, Morgan enables Chuck to find Sarah sitting on that Malibu beach in his. In a sense, the former "pip-squeak side-kick" not only grew over five years to a point where he could offer help to save others, but ultimately found that in the process he himself had been saved.

CHAPTER 20:

Prism Express

El Compadre. Wienerlicious. A dance at a formal gala and a heart-to-heart on that beach in Malibu. Before the curtain falls on "Chuck," viewers are returned to Season 1 for a virtual farewell tour, reminding them just how many adventures the Castle Couple shared... and just how much they both grew in the process. As nostalgic as the trip down Memory Lane may be, a more dramatic encore that returns Sarah and Chuck to earlier versions of themselves takes center stage to cast a pall over the series finale arc. By the time they take their bows, however, both Chuck and Sarah succeed in swiftly retracing their personal journeys involving deep-seated identity issues in time to share the promise of a life rediscovered together.

With the memory of the last several years wiped from her mind by the Intersect, the final pair of episodes in Season 5 largely focuses on Sarah's struggle to determine, once again, what is real and what is possible. This struggle begins with the most basic questions: Who am I? A spy or something more? Who is Chuck? An enemy or husband-lover? And do I trust anyone to help me discover the answers? On the conscious level, Sarah is actually returned to a mindset that pre-dates Season 1, bearing a far more similar resemblance to Ryker's distrustful "loner" and Graham's "wild card" than the better-adjusted, flirty-if-deceptive spy that brings Chuck a phone to fix in the pilot. Moreover, Quinn adds a thick layer of loathing by informing Sarah that Chuck is not, as in Season 1, simply a guy who may or may not be in league with an allegedly rogue Bryce Larkin, but a "traitor" personally responsible for the deaths of Bryce and Graham who poses a "major threat to national security." Her orders are more explicit, too: return the Intersect glasses and "kill Chuck Bartowski."

Sarah doesn't play any favorites in the trust game. Indeed, Quinn receives no more of Sarah's faith than anyone else at the outset, evidenced by Sarah throwing him out a hotel room window and dangling him by his tie, even though he claims to have been her handler for the last five years. Guarding him with gun in hand, her trust remains thin until Quinn selectively shows her the first report of her video log, which merely verifies her assignment to monitor Chuck almost five years prior. Even afterwards, her visual response to Quinn does not display complete confidence, a lack that continues to imply itself despite her insistence in the Intersect room that Quinn told her the truth about Chuck and the Castle crew. As Roan Montgomery earlier notes of Sarah in a different context, she doth protest too much.

Though armed with a massive prejudice against Chuck, in addition to the natural distrustful instincts of her past (see Chapter 2: Fish Out of Water), something lurks beneath the conscious level in Sarah's mind that disputes her surface thoughts and gives her pause in carrying out Quinn's orders. The first night in bed with Chuck upon her return home, after she thinks she has found the Intersect glasses and receives orders to "take out" Chuck, Sarah hesitates, lingering over Chuck's sleeping form until he awakes and the opportunity passes. A similar event occurs the next day. After betraying the Castle team in the Intersect room, she allows Chuck, who appeals, "It's me. It's your Chuck," to slowly approach her and lower her pistol-pointing arm before she recovers at Quinn's command and strikes him. Still, once outside the building she delays detonating the explosive she leaves and even suggests to Quinn that blowing it may not be necessary. And when Quinn pushes the button anyway, her punch to his jaw upon rejoining him suggests anger over something more than just, as she alleges, his destruction of a government facility.

Equally intriguing, Sarah twice returns to Chuck after realizing the truth about Quinn's treachery, despite denying any personal link to Chuck. As Chuck pointedly asks Jeffster just prior to Sarah ironically showing up at the Buy More, "How do you find a woman that doesn't want to be found?" You don't. So why does a disconsolate Chuck leaving Ellie's apartment turn to find Sarah standing in the courtyard? Did she really come, after apologizing, simply to announce her departure, perhaps forever? When that mission to kill Quinn fails, Sarah again returns to linger with her finger over the bell at the Nerd Herd desk, wearing an outfit curiously similar to that which she wore upon her arrival at the same desk in the pilot. Somehow sensing Chuck's presence a good distance behind her, Sarah turns to face him. But simply to ask if she can use his base? In both cases, Chuck asks the crucial question: "What are you doing here?" The repeated emphasis implies a reason deeper than her pretexts can fully provide.

This internal conflict between conscious and subconscious factions proves responsible for the emotional fortress Sarah re-erects to guard herself, though the walls briefly lower themselves on occasion. Before the revelation of Quinn's deception, these glimpses into her troubled heart are bookended by resistance. Two scenes in particular serve as almost exact mirrors of this pattern. In the first, set in Ellie's apartment, Chuck confides his concern for Sarah to Ellie while Sarah, following Chuck to the apartment, listens upstairs undetected. Sarah's initially guarded mindset is figured with the aid of the camera angle, which pointedly frames her from downstairs rounding the hallway corner through the balcony guardrail, head held rigidly and hand gripping the knife. A subsequent angle, shot from Sarah's perspective upstairs looking down on Chuck and Ellie, frames the siblings through the same decorative wrought iron. Accordingly, Sarah's demeanor remains hostile until the evocative soundtrack begins and Chuck unveils his hurt over his wife pulling her feet away in bed. During this segment, the guard rail is notably omitted from the frame. Ellie proceeds to empathize, "It's her first night back. Can't imagine what she's been through," when Quinn, via earpiece, asks Sarah what they are talking about. Sarah hesitates before replying, "About me," her jaw relaxing and the slight tremble of her lips matching that of her voice. As Chuck continues to lament the close call with losing his best friend and now his wife to the Intersect, he reveals his desire to destroy it, contrary to Quinn's assertion to Sarah, whose expression shifts from malevolent to distant. However, the moment Chuck prepares to return to his own apartment, the last shot the viewer receives of Sarah returns her behind the guard rail missing during the interim, her defenses resurrected.

The same dynamic plays out in the Dream House scene. Tied to the chair, Sarah begins with her emotional walls reaching the ceiling. After Chuck explains how her assignment to him began as a cover relationship

152

but developed into a real one, Sarah, calling him "Bartowski," flatly denies it with an expression a tad too bold, perhaps to negate her glassy eyes: "My job was to make you think I feel something…That's what I do best. I lie." But when Chuck calls her on it, claiming, "Actually, you're not as good a liar as you think you are," Sarah's fragile veneer strips away to expose doubt in a moment, her eyes averted. And as Chuck details moments of their love affair, Sarah continues to swallow back her emotion until, with tears streaming down Chuck's face, they begin to well in her own eyes. On the brink of internal collapse, Sarah manages to steel herself once again, initially with a touch of remorse, to say, "I'm sorry…I did my job too well." Within moments, Sarah is kicking him down the stairs…followed by the prominent focus of the camera lens on the moving silhouette of her shadow-self as she walks by the stairs' guard rail.

Incidentally, Sarah's penchant for lying as a self-defense mechanism ends up recalling another scene from Season 1 as well. After Sarah realizes the glasses she gives Quinn from the Intersect room upload are empty, she claims Chuck tricked her. On the surface, she angrily declares, "I made a mistake. I promise you I will not make that same mistake again." But has she? Won't she? When confronted by Chuck in "vs. the Crown Vic" after The Incident, Sarah used almost the exact words when attempting to avoid the reality of her feelings for him: "What happened was a mistake. One I will not make again." That certainly didn't turn out to be the truth. The same could be said of telling Chuck her impulsive decision to run with him in Prague was a mistake she will not make again (vs. the Pink Slip), for she also reverses that statement a dozen episodes later when poised to meet him at Union Station (vs. the American Hero).

While dealing with her psychological conflict, Sarah must increasingly process the testimony of others regarding her identity, and there is no shortage of it. Though these testimonies accent her subconscious tug towards Chuck, they only intensify her inner turmoil, because they point her in the direction of a truth made problematic by her amnesia. Held at gunpoint, Ellie earnestly identifies Sarah as a trusted family member who shared her most precious moments: her wedding and the birth of her daughter. Casey, who she remembers as a cold-blooded assassin, stops by her hotel room to confess, "I guess Bartowski's made us both a little soft," before enlightening her that they, former enemies, "changed" to forge a friendship together. These words are given further expression in the hearty hug she observes the "unfriendly, unforgiving" agent of the past initiate with Chuck in their farewell.

Then Morgan takes a turn in the witness stand. After releasing him from an instinctive mugging in Castle, Sarah hears him graciously testify, "...There was a time when I was Chuck's number one go-to best friend. And then you came along, and things changed. It's just that if I was to hand the title off to anyone, I was always really happy it was you." These verbal testimonies are reinforced by a home full of photos she peruses displaying her former life with Chuck. Can they all be lying? But that's essentially the problem: they communicate a truth threatening for Sarah to confront absent a memory to link it with or confidence in her ability to once again make it a reality.

Sarah has even more difficulty keeping Chuck's testimony in the Dream House from skirting her defenses, especially when Quinn's lies are revealed. As Chuck notes, *she* kissed *him*, a real kiss. Months and months of wandering later, when he had given up hope, a day came that she affirmed she loved him. Accepting a marriage proposal wasn't even an issue, because they both already knew they wanted to spend the rest of their lives together. They were going to raise a family in the Dream House together. She was happy. And not alone. Chuck concludes with a direct appeal, kneeling before her. The sincerity of his words as well as the transparency of his demeanor evoke emotions so strong that even Sarah the Cynic is left asking, "This is real? You love me?" in a moment of incredulous belief.

Still, these testimonies pale in comparison to the most credible witness of all: herself. Exhibit A is the carving she recognizes in the door frame of the Dream House. In an instant, her demeanor changes from steely spy to broken amnesiac, huskily admitting, "I wrote that." Sarah appears to relent on her execution order before Quinn enters and confirms the truth of his lie. Subsequently, Sarah watches the video logs that uniquely chronicle her personal journey with Chuck in a manner nothing can dispute. In the process, she transforms from a curious and perhaps still slightly skeptical spectator to one undeniably consumed with feelings.

The shift begins with a raised eyebrow over the angst apparent in her Wienerlicious dumping and continues with signs of confusion while watching her sheepish, I-still-can't-quite-believe-it admission that she kissed Chuck, confirming his Dream House story. The transformation becomes complete when Sarah views an internally dissolving Agent Walker of Season 2 stare into the lens to declare with whispery voice and without reservation, "I love Chuck Bartowski, and I don't know what to do about it." Barring the climax of "vs. Phase Three," the amnesia-plagued Sarah retains less emotional control at this moment than any other in the series: her hands instinctively reach to her lips and then to the throat below a mouth agape, her facial features contorted. Combined, the doorframe and the video log scenes hurtle Sarah into an emotional free fall that no fortifications can fully guard against, a dynamic figured on the heels of this scene in Sarah's plummet from Quinn's plane at the beginning of the final episode.

In the midst of this emotional plunge, Sarah struggles between two competing visions of herself: the independent spy Sarah Walker and the lover-wife Sarah Bartowski that emerges from the testimonies of her erased past. This double vision is dramatically imaged in Sarah's hotel room immediately after realizing Quinn's deception at the Dream House and before the arrival of Casey and the video log. Hurriedly packing to "run," as Chuck urged, the camera presents Sarah rushing back and forth between the counter in front of her wall mirror and the suit case on the bed. Each time she approaches the mirror, the lens catches both the real Sarah and the phantom one facing each other. But which is she?

In her mind, the span between the two is massive and seemingly unbridgeable. Sarah grants Chuck the most unguarded glimpse into her thoughts found in the finale arc when, on the verge of leaving for Berlin alone, she confesses, "I, I, I can't be here." Her eyes meet his with a hint of appeal in them, and her voice softens before she continues with a slight shake of the head. "I don't know how to be the woman you remember me as. All I remember is being a spy, a good one…It's all I know how to do." These words betray the fear of her perceived inability to bridge the gap between her past and present, if a future with Chuck is indeed a vision that still appeals to her. And if she does desire the vision of Sarah Bartowski, and musters the courage to risk attaining it, can she trust Chuck? Sarah's struggle to answer these questions will continue up to the end of the episode, when Sarah leaves Chuck behind at Castle for perhaps the final time, explaining, "I, um,…I need to go find myself….I need some time to think. To be alone."

Though Sarah's emotional walls remain in some form up to the beach scene, they no longer prove so imposing or impossible to scale after the doorframe and video log revelations. While watching the video logs, the viewer gains a private, unguarded look at an emotionally overwhelmed Sarah that indicates she is not entirely truthful in her next encounter with Chuck. When Sarah finds herself drawn to the courtyard to apologize to Chuck and say goodbye, she tells him that though she now believes everything he said she just doesn't "feel it." The video log aside, her mere presence and declaration about going after Quinn because he "took away my life" imply some level of contradiction to her statement. But her ironic demeanor further disputes her words: red and occasionally averted eyes; pursed lips; repeated swallowing; a voice that reaches a whisper. Sarah even lingers silently before walking away, as if longing for some additional response from Chuck before departing for something far more within her comfort zone: a spy mission to kill Quinn. Granted, Sarah certainly lacks the frame of reference, due to her amnesia, to fully recall her former love for Chuck, but the evidence confirms she is feeling something more than she admits. Not coincidentally, the camera pans back as Sarah leaves, allowing the frame to encompass the fountain... and the connotation-laden lily pads floating within (see Chapter 1: Water Lillies).

Sarah's first visit to Castle illustrates her weakened walls as well. After finding her mission to find Quinn will take her to Berlin, she pointedly grabs luggage from the rack, implying she will handle her emotional baggage on her own. And when Chuck asks what she will do when she gets there, she openly, even casually tells him she will kill him. Her manner changes, though, before she curiously proceeds to say, without Chuck's solicitation, "And then I disappear forever," her eyes suddenly averted. Is this statement a staged vehicle to gauge Chuck's reaction? Sarah's eyes remain on him as he, grasping for any means to keep her from walking out of his life, tells her he can help with her mission, noting, "With us, you stand a chance." Significantly, she accepts, implying she has not closed the door on the larger mission tied up with it: rediscovering who she really is with Chuck still part of that equation.

Perhaps due to this decision, Sarah's walls shrink further on the Berlin mission. At the El Compadre, Chuck is able to continue telling their story, that is until his charming transparency begins to outflank Sarah's defenses too quickly. Even while squelching the beginnings of a smile when hearing him recall her "crazy, sexy" dance moves on their first cover date, Sarah urges a refocusing on the mission, but with a new vitality evident in her tone. At the Russian consulate gala, the façade continues to dissolve. Accepting Chuck's compliment on her appearance, she gives one in turn and raises him one by initiating contact when straightening his tie and sneaking a glance into his eyes, just as Sarah safely took pleasure in grooming him in Seasons 1 and 2. Moreover, while they dance, signs of distraction and even attraction begin to appear, their mouths hovering near each other. And when she bids Chuck to "get me close," she seemingly has to remind both herself and Chuck that she means "to Rennie."

By the time they reach the Wienerlicious, an additional sign of hope appears. As the pair wipes down the tables, figuring her wiped-away memories, Sarah notes, "We have some waiting around to do," implying the time it will take for the memories to come back. Next, she muses, "The [cups are] in the wrong order…It's not how it should be," and feels compelled to rearrange them, ostensibly to match the typical configuration of the Wienerlicious in Season 1, though she claims no memory of the place. More important than merely a sign that her memories may be slowly returning, the action figures Sarah's emotional rearrangement as she considers a future with Chuck, just as she did in the opening scene of "vs. the Santa Claus" (see Chapter 7: Thunder and Rain).

Despite this, the trajectory of Sarah's emotional recovery is not strictly upward and onward. No sooner do they return to Castle after Chuck allows Quinn to escape, while shooting Casey's chopper down, than Sarah challenges Chuck's spy credentials before leaving to find Quinn yet again, this time without him. Only Mary Bartowski, with a gun and intelligence on Quinn, stops her from leaving. At the briefing, they notably sit apart.

In the final scenes at the concert hall, however, Sarah again cracks open her emotional gates. On the rooftop, after she guns Quinn down, Sarah looks searchingly into Chuck's eyes when he explains the plans to reinstall her memories with the Intersect glasses. Sarah asks, "Will it work?" suggesting her desire for the plan to succeed, as she does again when warning, "There's only one upload left." Her fallen expression reinforces that impression, and when Chuck pines to Sarah that he will now not be able to get her back, her appearance does anything but confirm that notion. Also noteworthy, Sarah subconsciously suggests using the Irene Demova virus to prevent the detonation of the bomb, even though she later admits she didn't know what she meant by it. Yet, when the bomb is diffused, Sarah, a model of conflict, skips the celebration and walks past Chuck, recalling a similar scene from Season 1 in "vs. the Nemesis" when she also masked feelings for Chuck. This turmoil continues through her final trek up the stairs at Castle, when she lingers one last time after Chuck affirms, "You have to go, and I understand."

Though the attention centers on Sarah in the series finale, Chuck also largely reverts to his former self. While lying in bed, distraught over Sarah's condition and a future without her, he tells Team Bartowski gathered around and even in his bed (that would be Morgan), "I'm back where I was before, alone in Burbank." Ellie disputes her brother's assessment: "You are not alone. You have us and you are not the person you were five years ago." Even Baby Clara supposedly agrees. Just as Sarah awakens from her unconscious free fall, the footage of which is pointedly interspersed with this scene, Chuck reawakens to his own potential. Remembering himself as the agent who brought down The Ring and Fulcrum, Chuck determines Sarah is "not out of my league." Even then, however, he struggles, like Sarah, with a question of two identities. When told to be himself in his quest to regain Sarah, he replies, "Which version of myself? Lord of the Nerd Herd or charming Charles Carmichael?"

A pair of images in the Castle scene figure Chuck's rendition of the emotional free fall. The moment Sarah notes she needs a ticket to Berlin and intends to disappear thereafter, the frame positions Chuck above a computer screen featuring a spinning lunar/desert landscape and repeats the image on a separate monitor at the very moment Sarah mulls over whether to let him accompany her to Berlin. This image is reinforced by the emphasis given to Chuck's receipt of Casey's Desert Eagle pistol, implying his noble attempt to carry on in spite of his empty, vacant life without Sarah. Thus, when Jeffster covers "Take on Me" to keep the bomb from detonating at the concert hall, it also serves as Chuck's hopeful anthem in regards to Sarah's ultimate decision regarding their future.

However, before they meet on the beach for the final scene, Chuck has already completed one journey. In following the higher calling in saving the crowd with the Intersect glasses instead of his personal interest, he demonstrates once again the quality of a hero by pursuing a good greater than himself. In doing so, he also realizes his potential vision of himself as Agent Charles Carmichael, figured in the still eye image inserted into the flash that mirrors the image of Sarah's eye inserted into her free fall sequence earlier.

Chuck's and Sarah's respective journeys finally lead them to the Malibu beach and the strains of "Rivers and Roads." However, prior imagery not only hints at the outcome long before their toes hit the sand but also the manner in which that outcome will be achieved. Water imagery saturates the episode in general and this scene in particular, signaling an impending baptism. After her free fall, not only does Sarah emerge dripping on to the dry land from her ocean immersion, further imaging a primordial evolutionary transition, but the scene of Chuck's realization of where to find Sarah notably images the water from the fountain frothing over his shoulder. Similarly, the initial perspective presenting Sarah sitting on the beach emphasizes the ocean, stretching from the lapping surf on the shore to the hazy horizon. These images work in concert with Sarah's snapping back to consciousness during her free fall in time to pull the rip cord of the parachute that will save her. In the midst of that fall, the screen also focuses on Sarah's eyeball as she awakens, indicating the forthcoming change in how she will view herself and the life she will choose to live.

However, the most textured metaphor preparing for the events on the beach is found in the bomb-diffusing sequence that reprises the pilot. Details matter here. When Chuck finally gets a look at the bomb, he notes that it is linked to an older model Prism Express laptop with a "tricky configuration," suggesting the emotional intricacies of the amnesia-plagued Sarah, who likewise mirrors the old version of herself. Sarah blindly suggests using the Irene Demova virus, an idea that Chuck praises as brilliant because it will "circumvent the system" and disarm the bomb, much as Chuck's charm navigated around Sarah's emotional walls in the past and will again to diffuse her inner turmoil. So why the specific model: the Prism Express? The precisely chosen name calls attention to Chuck's transparency throughout the final two episodes, part of what charms Sarah, while also suggesting that Sarah will pursue the vision of Sarah Bartowski by looking at herself through the prism of Chuck's selfless love for her when she can't recall or envision it on her own. And she takes the express route: a memory-wiped Sarah somehow manages to reach her decision to strive for a life with Chuck in the matter of a few weeks when it took years to reach that destination in the past.

Within this context, the pieces fall in place in Malibu. For a third time in the finale, Sarah returns to Chuck, gravitating to the beach by somehow sensing it "is important" to them, though she has no recollection of their first visit. When Chuck arrives, there is no evidence of surprise or irritation; Sarah accepts his greeting, "I was hoping you'd be here," almost as if she expects him. This time, though, they trade places relationally, figured in the reversal of their positions from the pilot: Chuck sits to her left, and she to his right. Sensing Sarah's essential struggle, Chuck tackles the critical issue head-on. "This is actually where you told me it was going to be OK. That I could trust you," he begins, adding, "And that's exactly what I'm doing now, asking you to trust me."

As Chuck speaks, Sarah remains silent, pondering his words as she studies his face with angled eyes, dearly seeking clues to confirm Chuck's trustworthiness, though her demeanor masks it. "Sarah, I don't want anything from you," Chuck continues. Sarah's features betray a little strain as her eyes begin to glass over. "I just need you to know that wherever you go, I will always be there to help you." Sarah's devoted husband becomes tight-lipped, a tremble wrinkling his voice. "Someone you can call, whenever." Even as she continues to gauge Chuck's expression with searching eyes, Sarah silently nods with pursed lips, the top briefly mugging the lower. Turning her head to more fully face Chuck, her welling gaze directly meets his for a moment, but Sarah still can't speak. "Trust me, Sarah!" Chuck pleads, "I'm here for you always."

Can she? Is he? In the silence, these thoughts likely flood Sarah's mind. She only 'met' the man a few weeks ago. But he wouldn't fight her, even after she kicked him down the stairs. He was willing to let her pull the trigger rather than live without her, declaring, "You can kill me…I will never hurt you." Then he instinctively took a bullet to save her life. And yet, he was willing to give it all up to save a packed concert hall. One final time, Sarah's eyes scan Chuck's face before a quiet sigh escapes from her slightly heaving shoulders and she turns to face the surf once again. "He changed me once," she must be thinking. "He's already changing me again. And what is the alternative?" No fewer than ten seconds elapse before Sarah finally breaks the wave-accented silence, a deliberate decision reached. And for a fourth time, Sarah returns to him: "Chuck, tell me our story." Chuck's tight-lipped grimace of a smile reveals his realization that in asking him to do so, Sarah has already determined to add chapters to it.

From this climactic moment, all that follows is denouement. The decision made, Sarah's tension evaporates, a peace washing like the surf across her face. As Chuck gladly begins to narrate their love affair, Sarah relaxes into a series of smiles, an uninhibited slap to his arm, and streaming tears that match her husband's. And by the time she wipes the last of them away, recalling her wiped memories, Sarah finds herself ready to move forward to make new ones at express speed.

After urging Chuck to reveal Morgan's "crazy idea" about the "magical kiss" with a playful laugh, Sarah turns suddenly earnest to interrupt a rambling Chuck and firmly instruct him to put the theory to the test. In the pregnant pause that follows, Sarah's countenance displays such self-assurance that even as her husband's banded hand reaches for her awaiting face, it is clear that Sarah Bartowski has already become something more than just a vision of her former self. And if history is any measure, she won't look back from the broad if hazy horizon they face together.

48956414R00094

Made in the USA
Lexington, KY
19 August 2019